**This book is to be returned on or before
the last date stamped below.**

A Hatful of Talent

BUCKINGHAM PALACE

1st December, 1993.

Dear Dr Wood

    I am commanded by The Queen to convey her warm thanks to you, the Governors, Staff and Students of the University of Luton for your kind message of loyal greetings, sent on the occasion of your ceremony held in St. Mary's Parish Church, Luton, to mark the inauguration of the University.

    Her Majesty was delighted to receive this message, and the copy of the commemorative brochure and order of service, and sends her best wishes to you for the success of the University.

Yours sincerely

(SIMON GIMSON)

Dr. Tony Wood.

A Hatful of Talent

The Founding of the University of Luton

Compiled by Tony Wood & Stephen Bunker

UNIVERSITY of LUTON PRESS, 1994

Published by the University of Luton Press
Park Square, Luton, Bedfordshire, LU1 3JU, UK

© 1994 University of Luton Press and contributors

ISBN 1 86020 000 1

First published 1994

Printed by Commercial Colour Press, London

Contents

Acknowledgements

The university gratefully acknowledges the assistance of the following without which the project could not have been undertaken.

CONTRIBUTORS
Current Staff/Governors/Fellows
Bill Aitken, *Faculty of Design & Technology*
Stephen Bunker, *Faculty of Humanities*
Keith Cook, *Director (Support Services)*
David Cooper, *Faculty of Applied Sciences*
John Hassell, *Faculty of Design & Technology*
Dai John, *Deputy Vice Chancellor*
Jessie Manley, *PA to Deputy Vice Chancellor*
Craig Mathieson, *Head of Marketing*
John Matthews, *Chairman, Board of Governors*
Pam Vachon, *Head, Student Administration*
Gerald Vinten, *Faculty of Business*
Sam Whitbread, *HM Lord-Lieutenant of Bedfordshire*
Tony Wood, *Vice Chancellor*

Former Staff/Students
Oscar Ballard, *Student*
Jim Clarke, *Deputy Director*
Val Dempsey, *Assistant Director*
Alan Geeson, *Head Librarian*
Fiona Howart h, *General Manager, Putteridge Bury Conference Centre*
Bob Oxtoby, *Deputy Director*
John Shine, *Dean, Faculty of Construction*
Roy Steed, *Director*

EDITORIAL AND DESIGN SUPPORT
University: Audrey Burton, Stephanie Crocker, Gill Lake,
  Patricia Murchie
Cover design: Angie Morgan
Editor/DTP layout: Roger Thomas
Photo layout: Victorily Design
Photographers: Ray Hearne, Mike Howarth, Terry Hughes,
  Eric Meadows, Mike Pierce, Roy Stares

OTHER ASSISTANCE
Luton Museum
Omni Reproduction Furniture

Foreword

SAM WHITBREAD (HM Lord-Lieutenant of Bedfordshire and
Honorary Fellow of the University)

I T IS PERHAPS unusual for a book to be written about a university within 18
months of its foundation; but then the University of Luton is no ordinary
university. Just as the town of Luton has moved from being a single-
industry town (almost entirely reliant in the 19th century on the straw hat)
to one with a wide range of industries ranging from heavy engineering,
through electrical goods manufacture to the food and beverage industry,
so has its university evolved in parallel with the needs of those industries.

Starting with the establishment of commercial and technical classes for
school-leavers in the 1890s, through the Modern School, the Technical
Institute and the Technical College to the Luton College of Technology,
College of Higher Education and, finally, in 1993, to the University of
Luton, this evolution has not been merely a cosmetic changing of names.
It demonstrates a gradual raising of educational standards to meet the
changing needs of young people and the local industries and businesses
that employ them.

Progress since 1989 has been breathtakingly fast, with the goal of meeting
the requirements of a polytechnic snatched away in 1992, to be replaced
by the more glittering prize of full university status. The achievement of
this goal came as no surprise to those who were aware of the single-minded
ambitions of the management and staff. By 1993 Luton had become the
largest higher education college in the country, with the highest growth in
the sector for three successive years. It had more students than half of the
established universities and was recognised as the most cost-effective
college or university in the UK, giving better value for money than any
similar institution.

Much has been made in this book of what was seen by Luton as the
battle for independence from the Bedfordshire Council between 1987 and
1989. I personally hope all this can now be put behind us and that the
whole county can recognise the University of Luton for what it is – a centre

of excellence serving the needs of both young people and Bedfordshire industry. Bedfordshire is indeed fortunate to be able to boast of institutions such as Cranfield Institute of Technology and the University of Luton, as well as the parts of the new De Montfort University based in Bedford. The county is too small to be able to afford the antagonism that has so often existed between Luton and the rest of the county. Educationalists and businesses alike need to get behind the county's centres of excellence, for without their support the regeneration of the county's industry and commerce will be that much more difficult – if not impossible – to achieve.

Introduction

TONY WOOD

I CANNOT NOW RECALL who first suggested a book about the evolution of higher education in Luton, but I can remember the date. It was April 1989, an auspicious month for those working in the then Luton College of Higher Education, marking as it did the beginning of independence for the college.

An epic, often bitter, struggle with the controlling authority, which had been followed with increasing incredulity by the local media had – from the college's point of view – been brought to a successful conclusion. The comment was made on the basis that "the story should be told".

Whilst reason enough to justify such an undertaking, I felt – rightly as it turned out – the greater chapter was still to come. Despite subsequently receiving many similar suggestions, I chose instead to file away my personal records and memories for a future occasion.

When it became clear, four years later, that Luton was to become a university town, I needed little encouragement to resurrect the idea. The era about to begin appeared of such significance, it seemed right to take stock and consider how we had arrived at our present position.

The book which has resulted does not reflect a rigorous and scholarly history of higher education in Luton. That remains the task of some future author, perhaps in celebration of a notable anniversary which lies ahead. Rather, it draws unashamedly on the subjective comments of many contributors, writing about events or happenings in which they have, or had, a specific interest.

Whilst we have done our best to check the veracity of the facts to which they refer, the reader must make due allowances for the inadequacies of memory, and also perhaps in some cases for the narrowness of the views expressed. We are, nevertheless, grateful to all those who have been prepared to devote the time and thought required to contribute to this compilation. We freely acknowledge the inevitability that important omissions will have occurred, both of events and of people, which may have been integral to past successes. For such omissions, we unreservedly apologise.

Notwithstanding these, and any other imperfections, I hope the impression gained reflects the essential contributions made by very many individuals to higher education in Luton. Without their determination, vision, and commitment, the new University of Luton could never have been founded.

Truly "A Hatful of Talent".

September 1994

Higher Education
in Luton, 1890–1960

STEPHEN BUNKER

THE UNIVERSITY OF LUTON is rooted in the history of technical education. Its development has paralleled similar processes elsewhere in England – notably in the changing age range and background of its scholars and its central position in the evolving relationship between learning and industry. Local circumstances have, however, served at times to fuel debate about the purpose and control of Luton's higher education institution and, arguably, to shape decisively its character.

The technical college, from which the university sprang, had its origins in the growing national awareness at the end of the 19th century that a deepening shadow was being cast on the UK's imperial complacency. This was manifested in many ways, not least in an appreciation that the country's international economic and political supremacy was being challenged by rivals from Europe and North America. Some of these rivals, the Samuelson Commission reported in 1884, possessed systems of technical learning that were superior to the UK's and were feeding their respective nations' economic drive.

In Luton in the last quarter of the 19th century education was the most bitterly debated issue confronting the town, focusing upon a titanic struggle for supremacy between two forces, largely representative of Anglican and Nonconformist opinion, as the pugnacious Vicar of St Mary's sought first to prevent the establishment of a secular School Board and then to stifle its effective operation. The Nonconformists, who in the early stages of the struggle benefited from the crucial support of the liberal-minded Vicar of Biscot, had largely succeeded in their aims of running an efficient School Board dedicated to the provision of non-sectarian learning in suitable facilities. These matters were concerned, however, with elementary education – up to the age of 13. No more thought was given to the needs of young people beyond this age.

Luton relied for its wealth on a single trade, the straw hat industry. This provided scope for the rapid accumulation of modest wealth and, such was its precarious nature, its equally rapid loss. The character of Luton's hat trade, with its distinctive cottage economy core, meant that scholarship was not regarded as of much consequence, and the town's council – even one or two of its mayors – included individuals who had been blessed with only the most rudimentary learning. A later holder of the office of mayor, H. O. Williams, recalled the "very incorrect spelling" being displayed in notices and advertisements in the windows of the town's principal hat factories. By the close of the 19th century, however, perceptions of the requirements of Luton's economic and educational structure were shifting significantly.

There was no co-ordinated strategy consciously linking the industrial regeneration of the town with a reassessment of the needs of its young people after school and the appropriateness of their skills for employment. It is striking, nonetheless, that those who campaigned with such startling success for the diversification of the town's industrial base were also those who simultaneously called for education provision to be established for young people who wished to continue their studies after leaving school and who desired to pursue a career in industry and commerce.

From the late 1890s, through to 1914, Luton threw off its reliance on the fickle fortunes of the hat trade, embracing a host of new firms and new industries in the process. Vauxhall, Kent's and SKF were just three examples of numerous companies, large and small, that were induced to relocate to the town as the result of a tireless campaign run under the official auspices of the New Industries Committee. A joint venture of the Borough Council and the Chamber of Commerce, this in practice relied on the initiative and dedication of a handful of individuals. One of these was F. W. Beck, a local solicitor possessing commercial experience, who was an activist within the Chamber of Commerce. To Beck can go the credit for suggesting the establishment of a joint New Industries Committee and it was he, in 1895, who advocated the establishment of commercial and technical classes for school-leavers, modelled on those operated by London County Council. Beck's view was echoed by a fellow Chamber member, hat factory manager and town councillor, J. H. Staddon, who expressed the opinion that "most lads leaving school were really of little use when they came into business, being quite unqualified for the work set them to do".

The extent to which the English were antipathetic towards the industrial ethos, notably as expressed in the prejudices of its educational establishment, is highly debatable. Less so is the historical inadequacy in the country's technical and commercial instruction. This was apparent at the outset when Beck sought to apply his principles to the existing educational apparatus in Luton. Under the Technical Instruction Act of 1889 the Bedfordshire County Council was empowered to provide grants for technical education, but Luton's application for financial support was refused. Relations between the industrial town and the rural county, dominated by Bedford, were rarely good. Indeed, Luton had long since ceased to feel any common bond with Bedfordshire, whose values, politics and economy were so very different to its own. There may, therefore, have been little expectation in the town that the county would show any interest. On the other hand there was neither infrastructure nor finance within Luton which could satisfactorily promote technical and commercial education. Even those who supported Beck, such as the Liberal *Luton News*, doubted whether the School Board was equipped to "afford much assistance in advancing the scheme" and subsequent events bore out these misgivings, mirroring failure at national level.

Beck's most powerful ally was the hat manufacturer Charles Warren, the embodiment of a contemporary Luton businessman: a sparsely educated man who, paradoxically, combined hard-headedness in commercial life with a liberality borne out of the Nonconformity in which he was immersed. A leading Borough Councillor, it was Warren who held all the threads in Luton's economic expansion, personally negotiating with companies considering relocation and liaising with the council and the Chamber of Commerce. Warren was also chairman of the School Board, with experience of supervising commercial and technical exams in the London system, and was better placed than any other individual to appreciate the limitations of Luton's apparatus. He, like the Chamber of Commerce, had hopes that the town's own Higher Grade School in Waller Street would act as a forum for a series of continuation classes and was probably the instigator of the establishment of a Technical Education Committee as an adjunct to the School Board. In addition, the Chamber of Commerce's secretary, Thomas Keens, wrote to all the schools in the town advocating the value of a commercial education scheme being formulated by the Chamber by September 1895.

It is no surprise that someone of Beck's temperament did not wish his scheme to be subject to the ponderous considerations of Luton's educational structure, the inhibited expenditure inclinations of the School Board and the parsimony of some of those in public life. If the School Board was ill-equipped to develop a system of further education, however, the Chamber was in an even worse position. Its own commercial examination, aimed at those at school as well as those who had left, was run under the overall supervision of the London County Council and exams were set for the following July. As an inducement, first-year enrolments paid no fees and prizes of £3, £2 and £1 were awarded to the most successful candidates.

Running parallel with this were the continuation classes organised by the School Board at Waller Street. The curriculum was broad to say the least, reflecting the unfocused, uncertain attitude toward further education and, no doubt, the particular interests of those running the classes rather than being based on a clear strategy designed to equip young people for a world beyond full-time school. Chemistry, dominoes, hygiene, drawing, botany and chess were the initial classes run (Beck wanted book-keeping but didn't get it) to which was added "domestic economy", a subject deemed suitable for girls and something of a patronising irony since the production of hats, in homes and factories, was overwhelmingly a female-dominated trade – at times a very well paid one. The continuation classes were pioneered by Warren who organised an initial meeting in Waller Street on 10 October 1895 at which W. Boston Bourke of the London School Board addressed a gathering of councillors, School Board members, education officials, teachers and interested individuals. From the outset Warren was keen to emphasise that the classes were for those returning to education as much as those who were continuing it.

The School Board's continuation classes were certainly more successful than the Chamber's technical classes at which attendance remained disappointingly low, although two pupils matriculated to London University in the first year. By July 1896 the scheme had run aground, to the regret of Beck, with no schools within the town prepared to promote it. Thereafter the Chamber saw its educational role as a promotional one, offering prizes for technical education run by other bodies.

The institutional antecedents of the University of Luton can be traced directly to the Luton Modern School, which was established in 1904 and from 1908 occupied the site now used by the present Park Square Campus of the University of Luton. its establishment followed the passing of the Balfour government's Education Act in 1902, which rationalised educational control, abolished the School Boards and established a more precise hierarchy of education authorities. Under the terms of the legislation, Luton was deemed to be a "Part III authority", responsible only for elementary education. The predominant education authority was now clearly Bedfordshire County Council, which was held responsible for all other matters, including higher education.

The County Council appointed T. A. E. Sanderson, MA, an ex-military man, as the first headmaster of Luton Modern School. Sanderson, a ferocious disciplinarian, known as "Timmy" behind his back – although certainly not within earshot – was responsible not only for the Modern School but also, as Principal, for a Technical Institution housed in the same building. The Modern School, which was established as a co-educational body, educated its pupils up to the age of 16 and had a curriculum which strongly reflected Sanderson's preference for maths and science. By 1907, 360 students were being taught in the Technical Institution across 28 subject areas. These varied from French and German to shorthand, dressmaking, book-keeping, carpentry and joinery, and home nursing. The number of scholars going on to take examinations was disappointingly low: just two from a class of 21 who were taught elementary French, for example.

This arrangement succinctly exemplified the lowly national position of vocational higher education in general and technical/commercial study in particular. Courses at Park Square were not well organised, but for those who went to other Luton schools the situation was even worse. The Technical Institution admitted its scholars at 16, fine for Modern School leavers but potentially disastrous for others in the town who were only taught up to the age of 14 and had to grope their way through a muddled system of inadequate classes before they were of an age to be admitted to the Institution.

The Workers' Educational Association, formed in 1903 to fill some of these gaps, established a branch in Luton in 1910, whilst at a national level the woeful state of education beyond elementary level was challenged by Frank Pullinger, an official at the Board of Education. Pullinger identified the failure of higher education, particularly with regard to technical learning, when in a 1909 report he complained that "insufficient attention is focused upon trades and industries and their related educational needs". Pullinger called for the expansion of continuation classes to fill what was described as the "fatal gap" between school and work. Although technical instruction was restructured in the years between 1910 and 1913 both it and science fell far short of educational and economic needs, and were very much the poor relation when compared with the traditional universities, the grammar schools and the humanities.

This shortcoming especially needed addressing in an industrial town such as Luton which had deliberately embraced new and rapidly expanding engineering companies. The history of the Luton Technical Institution, later the Technical College, up to the completion of the Park Square site in the early 1960s, is one of constrained expansion outgrowing the limited facilities available in the Modern School, in response to the enormous demand from people drawn (in the main) from trade and industry.

Notwithstanding this demand, the college was to be the last to acquire purpose-built accommodation. The girls of the Modern School were separated from the boys and acquired their own site with the establishment of the Luton High School for Girls in 1919. The boys moved to their own buildings in Bradgers Hill Road in 1938 (an establishment soon renamed Luton Grammar School) and the Secondary Technical School moved to Barnfield Avenue in 1958. Within the national context of insufficient commitment to vocational training, the Technical Institute grew rapidly in order to try to match the demand of the new engineering firms: these were expanding at a prodigious rate in a locality which has been described as the least depressed town in the UK during the inter-war period. Within that local context, however, there were certainly some within the town who perceived the Technical Institute to be insufficiently resourced by Bedfordshire County Council, a lack of commitment that seemed apparent from the unsuitable Modern School building on Park Square.

This criticism is difficult to sustain. While there is little doubt about the shortcomings of the Technical Institute's accommodation, sole control by the Borough would not necessarily have made any effective difference. As it was, the governing body of the Technical Institute overwhelmingly consisted of Luton-based individuals who were representative of local politics, education and industry. Under the chairmanship of Hedley C. Lawrence, a Labour councillor who had experience of being both employee and employer in the building trade, work began on an extension to the rear of the Institute in 1936, the name of which was formally changed in May 1937 to Luton Technical College. The ill-fated extension was known as the Jury Building or Jury Block, after its Bedford designer, and although envisaged to cover 125,000 square feet it was still incomplete when the outbreak of the Second World War halted work. In the meantime students continued to use eight temporary wooden huts in lieu of their purpose-built accommodation. At this time there were only around 50 day-release students.

Hedley Lawrence's successor as chairman of the governing body in 1937 was John Burgoyne, a man whose manners, values and political beliefs were redolent of the Edwardian era rather than the one in which he was to play a major role. Burgoyne, born in 1875, had inherited his father's hat business but had retired in 1926 in order to pursue a public career, in particular his real passion – the cause of learning. Both a Borough and a County Councillor, Burgoyne served on the Bedfordshire County Council Education Committee from 1934 and eventually became its chairman, a position he held for 13 years. He became involved with most aspects of education in Luton, and with particular institutions such as Luton Grammar School, but it was his devotion to Luton College of which he was probably most proud. This was a dedicated service which was second only in importance and fond memory among Lutonians to his outstanding tenure as Mayor between 1938 and 1944. Burgoyne was knighted in 1955, a move regarded locally as being for services rendered in wartime and education. Arguably a more fitting epitaph for his service, though, would have been for substance to be lent to the proposal that the new Park Square building be named after him.

Burgoyne's assumption of the chair coincided with the appointment of W. E. Park as the new Principal of the College. Park, whose entire institution was now dedicated to technical learning, strengthened the links between

Luton College and industry. The public figures on the governing body (many of whom came from a commercial background in any case) were joined by representatives from industry, most notably Charles Bartlett, who, as Managing Director of Vauxhall, decisively shaped not merely the structure of Luton's premier industry but also the character of the whole town. The expertise on the Governing Body was augmented by an Engineering Advisory Committee representing George Kent's, SKF, Commer Cars, Hayward Tyler and Vauxhall. However, there were still just four full-time lecturers (C. W. Tonkins being Senior Lecturer in Engineering) the rest being classified as "visiting teachers". Engineering, and to a lesser extent Building, dominated the curriculum, which ranged from foundation courses through to City and Guilds and the Higher National Certificate which, with the Ordinary National Certificate, had been introduced in the 1920s. Courses considered suitable for women were not forgotten in the more than 130 classes: to the Dressmaking and Household Cookery organised as "Women's Classes" was now added More Advanced Cookery at which was taught the making of choux pastry and Christmas cakes, and grilling.

"If we do not provide the best technical education . . . this country is sunk, because we will not be able to compete in world markets or anything else" warned W. F. Stephenson, Park's successor as Principal, to an audience of apprentices in 1953. Stephenson, who became Principal in November 1952, was echoing an old sentiment which was recognised considerably beyond local boundaries but which again was reckoned to be one not matched by action, a feeling that became stronger as it became apparent that post-war economic growth in the UK was lagging behind that of competitors for world markets such as Germany, France and Japan. This even though the Butler Education Act of 1944 gave added impetus to further education, requiring all education authorities to provide a facility for this and providing increased grant provision in the process. This marked the commitment on the part of central government to intervene, being followed in 1945 by the Percy Report, which further highlighted the need for the expansion of technical education as well as the need to elevate its status. To a certain extent this had been undermined rather than enhanced by the Butler Act which created a tripartite system of schooling – grammar, secondary and technical – the latter two swiftly coming swiftly to be regarded as the poor relations, recruiting those who failed to pass the 11+ examination and thus go on to a grammar school.

Luton Technical College was not designated a College of Advanced Technology under the scheme initiated by the Conservative Government in 1956 and thus was to miss out on an early opportunity to achieve university status. It nonetheless grew rapidly in the post-war era, driven in particular by the demand from local industries which had expanded under the exigencies of the Second World War and continued to do so thereafter. These firms, above all Vauxhall, provided an almost insatiable demand for the products of an institution whose inadequate accommodation was plain for all to see. The largest proportion of scholars by far were part-time students pursuing vocational qualifications, an increasing number of whom attended on day release from their employers, an arrangement which succinctly illustrated the college's relationship with local business and the specifically parochial emphasis of its strategy.

In 1948, after discussion with the Ministry of Education, the building plans of the 1930s were shelved, with the third phase (out of four projected) almost complete. Instead, a new purpose-built college was to replace all that then stood on the Park Square site. These plans were at no more than the approval stage when the easing of government controls and more expansionist economic policies led to a dramatic increase in students in the mid-1950s: 3,500 enrolments in 1952 were followed by a 1,500 increase by the September of the following year. Narrow corridors and basements were utilised as overflow classrooms as waiting lists grew, and the press dubbed the embarrassed home of further education the "Pack-Em-In-College". This "pitiable" situation for students endeavouring to pursue courses such as carpentry and joinery or machine-shop engineering in overcrowded, outdated facilities was thrown into a starker light by the opening of the new Hatfield Technical College in September 1953. This institution a few miles away in Hertfordshire offered a broader curriculum as well as courses which seemed to rival Luton's to the point of even threatening to poach students from the town. In reality, demand was so great that this fear was never realised although Hatfield was to become regarded in some ways as a competitor of Luton College.

In May 1954 the contractors, Y. T. Lovell and Sons Ltd, at last began work on the new buildings to accommodate the Luton and South Bedfordshire College of Further Education (to give it its recently acquired full title) signalling the end to what a frustrated Burgoyne had described as a long "exercise in the theory of negativity". Phases I and II of the development snaked around the existing buildings used for the college while compulsory purchase orders cleared room in Park Square and Church Street, removing shops, the Pentecostal Church (after some wrangling over compensation) and The Wheatsheaf public house, a hostelry whose place in Church Street was a reminder of Luton's pre-industrial era. The foundation stone was laid, appropriately enough by Burgoyne, on 4 May 1955 in the presence of Hedley Lawrence (serving as Mayor that year) and a former student of the Institute, Sir Frederick Mander, who had succeeded Burgoyne as the chairman of Bedfordshire Education Committee. An overjoyed Burgoyne recalled the hesitant development of Luton College to this stage declaring "God bless the development of this College and all who should work and learn here".

The exultancy of Burgoyne, Lawrence and others, who were beginning to see the fulfilment of many years' plans, schemes and dreams, was not automatically matched by those who had to work and study in an inadequate building, now compounded by the disruptions of living on a construction site, or alternatively, at either 32 Guildford Street or Beech Hill Girls School. Within a timetable which was operational from 9am to 9pm the number of students leapt to 6,000 in 1955's enrolment and by a further 800 the following year. Stephenson complained: "We are very badly off indeed for staff . . . many of our classes are twice as big as they should be," adding that it was proving difficult to recruit suitable lecturers, who could obtain far higher salaries in the private sector. To partly overcome this difficulty the Head of Engineering, F. Metcalf, secured the release of eight lecturers from local companies on temporary contracts.

Phases I and II of what Burgoyne described as the "wonderful" new building were ready for use by Easter 1957 and this was followed the same year by an application for new departments, Stephenson being only permitted one initially (Electrical Engineering), and an increase of staff from 77 to 86. By 1960 the number of academic and administrative staff totalled 134, a figure that did not include the vast army of visiting lecturers. These were serving eight departments: Mechanical and Production Engineering; Electrical Engineering; Commerce, Management and Liberal Studies; Science; Mathematics (added 1959); Building; Domestic Subjects; plus the School of Art ensconced in a penthouse on top of the engineering block.

Stephenson assiduously cultivated relations with industry, continuing the work of Park, by compiling an intricate array of advisory committees, each with its own distinctive structure, to serve subject areas. The Engineering Advisory Committee in 1960 comprised two college governors, three representatives of the Engineering and Allied Employers, one from the Eastern Electricity Board, one from Vauxhall, one from the Amalgamated Engineering Union, one from the Confederation of Shipbuilding and Engineering Unions and two co-opted members. By contrast the Commercial Department's Advisory Committee consisted of governors (two), Luton and District Chamber of Trade (one), Luton Junior Chamber of Commerce (one), Luton Industrial Co-operative Society (one), Bedfordshire, Buckinghamshire and Hertfordshire Group of the Society of Chartered Accountants, and Luton and District Clerical Workers Union (four).

The courses offered by the college, whose name changed again in 1958

11

to Luton College of Technology, were given a new dimension following a Government White Paper on Technical Education in 1956. This recommended the development of "sandwich" courses, periods of study by students at technical colleges alternating with their spending time at their places of employment, leading to degree qualifications. Luton had, in fact, already been preparing its own programme in conjunction with local employers. Upon approval of the Ministry of Education scheme, however, the college embraced the proposals, which one employer described as "an excellent and fair means of providing further education of a high academic standard for the quite sizeable group of boys able to profit by it".

The College's Assembly Hall was completed in 1959, providing an invaluable additional facility to a town bereft of an adequate concert hall. With Norman and Dawbarn's two-phase construction ready for occupation the old, now redundant buildings were demolished: the Modern School centred upon the hall from which Sanderson could survey his domain in the classrooms around and above, and the never-finished Jury Block, a "fine building" in "very good condition" according to Leslie Bowles of Luton's Committee for Education. Although there were considered to be strong architectural grounds for their subsequent demolition, the new college was only just large enough to meet current demand with, by 1961, the Head of Science confessing that Park Square was "rapidly reaching saturation point" and students were still having to be sent to Beech Hill School. Demand for engineering and secretarial courses rose by between 20 per cent and 50 per cent as these established subjects ran alongside new areas such as Management Studies or media courses (students developed their own TV studio) providing an overwhelming imperative behind Phases III and IV of the College building programme, the latter stage being finally completed in 1968. At this point, "the million pound college" envisaged in the early 1950s had cost £1,969,482.

The scale of the operation at Luton Technical College by the early 1960s would probably have greatly impressed Beck, Warren or Sanderson. Stephenson could refer with justifiable pride to the "magnificent" relations between industry and education which met in a relationship of mutual benefit on Park Square via the students who studied in evening classes and on day release and block release. In other respects the UK was far from being governed by what Sir John Wolfenden described as a "technocracy of learned men in white coats" and the euphoria around Harold Wilson's promise for the "white heat" of technological revolution was to evaporate soon after the election of a Labour government in 1964. Contrary to what Wolfenden claimed, young people did "care a jot about a white collar job" and impressive though Luton Technical College may have seemed its development had barely been commensurate with economic development

12

within the town as a whole. Student hours taught at the college increased tenfold between 1937 and 1961, but the population of the town as a whole had grown from around 90,000 to 131,505, with Vauxhall, SKF, Electrolux, Laporte and Kent's all more than doubling their workforce: Vauxhall's combined Luton and Dunstable plants alone employed approaching 20,000 workers. Impressive though the college certainly was, arguably even serving (in the words of Stephenson) as "a pattern" for the rest of the country, it could only just match demand against a national backdrop where failure to provide high-quality vocational training in sufficient quantity remained a problem which needed to be repeatedly addressed.

How It All Began

OSCAR BALLARD ("Student No. 5")

AT THE TENDER AGE of 13, while seated at our cast-iron framed oak desks at Denbigh Road Senior Elementary school one day in 1937, we found ourselves being addressed by a friendly figure of a man, Mr W. E. Park, the Principal of a brand new college in Luton – Luton Technical College. As part of this college, a Junior Technical School was to be formed, and we were invited to sit an entrance exam for the first intake. We were told that we would be destined, upon leaving, to be part of a group which had been conditioned in the ways of engineering, and thus would be suitable to take up apprenticeships at local firms, of which there were quite a number at the time.

Having sat the entrance exam, the successful students were called for an oral exam and interview. The first student group thus formed comprised the first 40 which began the JTS. We were divided into two forms; classes of 20 students were the exception at this time and half the size of those of our previous schools. We were to undertake a two-year full-time course covering 16 subjects, with internal exams at the end of each term. The facilities at Park Square possessed a newly constructed engineering block, including a well-equipped machine shop, drawing office, engineering science lab and heat engines lab. We shared a woodwork shop with the outgoing Luton Modern School which had been on the site for a number of years and was being relocated to Bradgers Hill. During the second year we took over the whole of the Modern School building and were joined by the Commercial School, consisting largely of girls. Our social life improved but our work probably suffered!

The end of the two-year course in 1939 coincided with the outbreak of the Second World War, and the local firms, uncertain of their future role, were going slow on taking on apprentices. This left 11 students without placements in employment, so a third year course was hastily cobbled together. Once finally in employment, students returned to the Luton Technical College for study towards the National Certificate and Higher National Certificate in mechanical engineering, usually on half-day release plus one evening. The brightest of the students achieved the HNC in four years – but due to my ineptness at exam passing it took me six! During this time the college had gone from strength to strength, being fuelled by an endless supply of students from JTS and others gathered along the way. Buildings arose and were later demolished as planners changed their minds and requirements developed.

At this point, many of us who were starting to take our future careers seriously realised that our options for further study were limited by the structure of the system. To return to the academic route would have meant backtracking and starting from scratch since there was no external school-leaving exam at the end of the original JTS course.

The option to proceed to a university degree was therefore all but closed. The alternative was to build up sufficient additional qualifications to enable application for Chartered Engineer status to be obtained. At this point in history, the major engineering institutions were accepting HNC plus industrial admininstration endorsements as the minimum qualification for Corporate membership. Thus the absence of an engineering degree was not too much of an embarrassment. Due to a quirk of the system in which the Royal Aeronautical Society allowed this grade to be achieved by the age of 25, (against 27 for the Institute of Mechanical Engineers) the writer had the good fortune to be the first student from the original group of 40 to become a Chartered Engineer.

Present-day students who aspire to this grade will probably find that they have to follow the academic route to a university degree, which of course they can now do locally. Although a degree is a stand-alone qualification. I would still recommend membership of the appropriate institution, as it shows dedication to the profession and encourages continuous career development. I am very much against any barriers which prevent a person from developing his career as far as his talents will allow – thus a system which allows a degree to be built up in modules would seem to fit this philosophy, particularly since engineering is more and more a multidisciplinary profession.

Once established in a career in engineering it was interesting to look back at the ways in which the Luton Technical College had helped me. First, in the JTS with its sound grounding in the relevant subjects. Second, the keen interest taken by engineering department Head, Mr D. A. Clark, to whom I shall always be grateful for arranging my employment by the Napier Company which lasted 30 years, and involved many interesting assignments overseas. Third, for the facilities to study engineering to an advanced level while in employment, enabling my qualification *objectives to be achieved. Finally, in later life, as a result of the wide range of courses available at later manifestations of Luton College – subjects as varied as computers, men's keep fit, amateur radio, photography and adult education teaching – enabled an update and diversification of knowledge to be obtained.*

It is with some sense of pride and satisfaction that one sees Luton College achieve university status and all students from those early beginnings wish it, and all present students, well for the future. To say that the college touched our lives would be an understatement – it made our lives, helped by that element of luck of being in the right place at the right time, and being assisted by the right folk. Present students have different hills to climb and different challenges to meet, but rest assured one day you will look back with satisfaction when you write your story on the University of Luton's 50th anniversary! ■

Memories of the 1950s

JOHN SHINE

RECRUITMENT OF STAFF to Luton College was a major problem in the mid-1950s. There was relatively full employment and college lecturers' starting salaries were on average £750 per annum, which did not bear comparison with what was available in industry and commerce. This meant that heads of department and the Principal tended to snap up potential staff members at short notice on the basis of instant personal decisions. The problem became so acute that the then Principal, Frank Stephenson, made annual recruiting trips to Huddersfield Technical Teacher Training College, one of two technical teacher training colleges. There he would interview students early on in their courses and offer them appointments before they had viewed the scenic delights of Luton or come to appreciate the inadequacies of the college's building. While not exactly being discouraged from visiting the college before agreeing to take up appointments, they were not issued with free rail warrants either.

The general shortage of lecturers in technical subjects – particularly engineering – was compounded in Luton because it was a boom town with a wide diversity of industrial and commercial firms. In order to help overcome this problem, Bedfordshire County Council had agreed that students appointed from technical teacher training colleges could be appointed by Luton College with effect from 1 July, immediately after their courses finished at the end of June. This meant that after two weeks at the college, mainly writing annual student reports to employers, they then started their careers with seven weeks of holiday/preparation. As a further incentive to attract teachers from disciplines where it was particularly difficult to recruit (mainly in engineering) the county council agreed that some could be appointed immediately to the second tier of the lecturer grade (Lecturer Grade B – Lecturer Grade A being the lower grade). During this period the Bedfordshire County Council was very supportive of the college both financially and in representing its interests at a national level.

At this time the college's physical resources were a stark contrast to the incentives given to its new staff. Some work had been done during the early part of the Second World War on the unfinished building in Park Square. It had a fine basement which had been reinforced to act as an air-raid shelter for the people of the town, and this was temporarily divided up to form 12 classrooms: these facilities were dubbed the dungeons by the staff. Apart from these, part of the ground and first floors provided just a few teaching units, and enterprise coupled with necessity had resulted in four wooden huts being constructed on top of the dungeons; even the two end corridors of the main building were used as classrooms. A feature of the building was the impressive metal lettering above the entrance – "Luton Technical College" – which would become an accurate title in the future but not so then.

A priority for new staff was a street map of the town so that they could locate the many college outposts. Teaching sites included the crypt at the Methodist Chapel in Guildford Street (since demolished) which was used as a plumbing workshop; the old Fire Station in Church Street, which has also made way for a new development; the Central Mission Hall, close to Luton Station; the Baptist Chapel opposite what is now the university site in Park Street; rooms above British Home Stores in George Street; the Luton Boys' Club in Park Street, a favourite with the students; the whole use of two former hat factories in Guildford Street, one simply referred to as 32 Guildford Street, and the other Hubbards, which was adjacent to the Wheelwright Arms public house (Hubbards was unusual, the college brickwork shop was on its second floor). Also used were a small office building next to Luton Town Hall and rooms in the Masonic Hall opposite the present university site.

On the Park Street site were two temporary wooden huts erected in a corner of the playground of the Luton Junior Technical School which shared the site with the college but was in effect the main landlord. By means of unclear negotiations and other agreements, part of the college was housed in the Luton Junior Technical School's main building on Park Square. The school was scheduled to move to purpose-built premises at Barnfield (buildings that now form part of Barnfield College). The School of Art occupied the whole of the top floor of the school while part of the college appeared to have a life of its own with a Headmaster, Mr Cyril Skinner. Some facilities, such as the school's woodwork shop, were shared with the college. This operation at times produced quite hilarious results – when students were erecting structures overarching the shop. Later, use was made of St Mary's Hall for teaching.

At this time the college had a public house within its grounds – the Wheatsheaf. It was situated in a sort of demilitarised zone between the Junior Technical School and the area deemed to belong to the college on the strength of the wooden huts erected in the school's playground. Beer deliveries entailed entering the playground in full view of the students in the huts who were wont at times to give forth a spirited cheer when they saw the draymen. As in all colleges, one or several local pubs became informal information or disinformation centres and the Wheatsheaf and, to a lesser extent the Red Lion, fulfilled this function. The pub was rather cramped and this aided the flow of information. With practically all the staff relatively new to teaching and technical education there was a lot to discuss. With just one small staff room catering for the whole of the 45 or so staff, the Wheatsheaf acted as an overflow. There was consternation when the Wheatsheaf was demolished to make way for the new college buildings.

After this the main college pubs were the Greyhound (later also demolished) at lunchtime and the Melson Arms in the evenings. The last of the true college pubs was the Black Bull in Park Street which became popular because it was close to the college and served good meals at a time when the college had no proper catering facilities. Its importance to the college steeply declined with the opening of college refectories, the provision of staff rooms, the increase in staff numbers and fragmentation into departmental enclaves.

Bill Johnson's Cafe next to the Masonic Hall was also a popular college venue, particularly when the only "official" facilities were those made available by the Technical School on a shared basis at lunch times – this meant sharing with school pupils. The scene here was reminiscent of a Hollywood prison film with rows of long trestles and wooden platform seats. The diners had identical trays and teachers patrolled around to ensure good behaviour. The school dinners at that time had not been scrutinised by dieticians so most staff made other arrangements. For some this meant Bill Johnson's Cafe.

Bill Johnson's was in a sense an unofficial part of the college. Not exactly a greasy spoon, for it was clean and the food was rather plentiful and wholesome, but no effort was made to impress by the decor. Bill Johnson handled the cash, served and was an informed college observer. The college staff occupied an area they had claimed for themselves. Even when the college possessed good catering facilities some stayed with him, but the building of the Arndale Centre put paid to the Cafe.

Being theoretically housed in one staff room and not dispersed by departments, the staff got to know each other well and problems were viewed on a college rather than departmental basis. This was reinforced by staff joining together in long treks to the far corners of the town or meeting each other at crossover points; to be late for your class in those circumstances was not a capital offence. It was often very difficult, though, to find anyone, even students. One sometimes encountered a bemused lecturer searching for his class in the wrong hat factory in Guildford Street. And because of the odd places in which one was required to teach odd scenes were to be expected. At the Central Mission a tune on the piano was a not unusual greeting and the Boys' Club offered scope during tea breaks for up and coming Steve Davises.

In 1955 the Principal was W. F. Stephenson and the heads of department were: Engineering, Frank Metcalfe; Building, Frank Talbot; Science, Nora Boothman; Commerce, D.G. Lintern; Mathematics, Henry Horner; Headmaster School of Art, Cyril Skinner; Registrar, J. H. Jeffs; and Deputy Registrar John Knowles. The non-teaching administrative staff totalled five, all housed in rooms in the Technical School.

The student numbers expanded each year and far outstripped the accommodation available. To overcome this problem entrepreneurial forces came into play in a type of 20th-century land grab or, more accurately, building grab; the town was scoured for yet more accommodation that could be used for teaching and further inroads were made into the Technical School. This was the period when the infamous 5pm to 7pm classes were started to ease the problem by another route. Many courses were of an evening-only type and the college premises were fully used from 9am until 9pm, and frequently 9.30pm; there was no Friday afternoon problem.

During this period, keeping registers up to date was considered the most important part of record-keeping since the financial viability of the college depended on it. At one time the Building Department neglected to keep registers for the Higher National Certificate in Building, and so the Head of the Department was a little perturbed halfway through the session to be asked by the Department of Education & Science to send them in for an unspecified purpose. However, registers were submitted having been compiled using different pens and handwriting, the whole being well fingered and spiced with a sprinkling of dust.

A few days later a letter arrived from the DES stating that these were copies and requesting the originals. There was now cause for concern and not just in the Building Department. Despite long sessions in the Red Lion no satisfactory solution was arrived at. Frank Stephenson was away that week and the prospect of presenting him with this problem caused considerable concern; Stephenson was not known for his toleration of incompetence.

When Frank Talbot eventually explained the situation to Stephenson, he was relieved that he seemed unconcerned, merely stating that bureaucrats at the DES did not start until 10am – come back at 10.30am.

At 10.30am Stephenson used the attack solution on the civil servants. My Head of Department, he claimed, is teaching 28 hours, is short of staff, has an extra intake of students and all his staff are working overtime, they have the college statistical returns to do, the college is awash with visits from HMIs, and as regards their comment that we had sent copies – of course we did, what if they had been lost in the DES organisation? He was prepared to consider the issue closed now that they had the figures – to this they agreed. While surprised by the solution, Frank Talbot was not surprised by what Stephenson had to say to him afterwards.

The main event of the year was the annual prize and awards day. This was started by Frank Stephenson and a notable feature was the eminence of the prize-givers. They included Dr Geoffrey Fisher, the Archbishop of Canterbury; Dr Donald Coggan, then Bishop of Bradford and later Archbishop of Canterbury; and the Headmaster of Eton College, Anthony Chenevix-Trench. The latter departed with Frank Stephenson's overcoat, which was returned by taxi from Eton.

The organisation had its hilarious side, eagerly anticipated by the staff sitting in the main hall. Each year there were well over a hundred awards ranging from certificates to boxes of spanners, these being awarded to students by department. The Heads, just prior to taking their seats on the stage, were given an amended prize list which was allegedly up to date, the students supposedly in sequence to match it.

On quite a few occasions this was not the case – a woman on an Architectural Technician course might receive a pair of Stilson wrenches and a Plumbing Certificate. Biologists would be awarded books on geology, and on one occasion a student expecting a top company award of a gold watch was presented with a certificate attributing to him a skill he did not know he possessed. Names were called out from the Heads' list and to add to the farce each student would be photographed by a local press photographer while being presented with the wrong award.

Another major occasion was the college's annual dinner and dance at the George Hotel in George Street (now demolished). Practically all the staff attended, as did a wide spectrum of Bedfordshire's persons of influence. As a new appointee to the Building Department I looked upon this as a good opportunity to meet friends and influence people. At the end of one such occasion two building employers, owners of large building companies, decided as a helpful gesture to assist Frank Stephenson – a Scotch drinker of note – to his car, aligned each side for support. In the crowded foyer, Frank, in a voice louder than usual, said: "I don't need you to hold me up, I don't fall down like your buildings." This was not exactly Dale Carnegie but fortunately from Frank it was acceptable – at least it appeared to be.

A HATFUL OF TALENT

At other special functions and awards the drink of the day was sherry. It is difficult with hindsight to think why wine was not used as an alternative, but sherry it was. This was not the first choice drink of a minority and the problem was overcome by decanting Cutty Sark Scotch, which has the same colour as pale dry sherry, into an empty sherry bottle. The Registrar at that time, John Knowles, would have a bottle in each hand and pour according to known preference. In a moment when his attention was deflected, a lady councillor of sober temperament detached the Scotch bottle from the Registrar in a gesture of assistance and, before composure was regained, poured herself and others the stronger beverage. There was no reaction and no comment – at least not from them. ■

From London External to CNAA Approval

DAVID COOPER

EXPANSION WAS THE order of the day in British higher education in the 1960s. Joining Oxbridge, London, the old Scottish universities and the redbricks were the so-called new universities (East Anglia, Essex, Kent, Lancaster, Stirling, Sussex, York and Warwick) and other universities that emerged from older institutions, particularly Colleges of Advanced Technology (Aston, Bath, Bradford, Brunel, City, Heriot-Watt, Keele, Salford, Strathclyde and Surrey). The proposals for polytechnics were also formulated, and by 1971 there were more than 30 of these degree-awarding institutions in the UK. Luton missed out on this burst of activity, being left as the largest town in the UK with neither a university nor a polytechnic.

In the early 1960s the Staff Association annual dinner and dance was an occasion when the Principal of Luton College, Frank Stephenson, took the opportunity to invite guests from business, industry and politics. The January 1965 event was the last to be held in the George Hotel before preparations began for the building of the Arndale Centre. Although remembered chiefly for the disproportionate length of time taken up by speeches (as another contributor to this book recalls), it should also be remembered for a speech by Luton's Labour MP, Will Howie (now Baron Howie of Troon), promising a university in Luton. Like many political promises, it took a long time to come to fruition and even then Luton had to wait longer than many other towns. Will Howie even suggested Stockwood Park as a possible location for the campus but the development of the Airport and the Stockwood golf course rather put paid to that idea.

The first degrees – the London years

In the 1950s and, despite new universities, the early 1960s there was a major shortage of degree-level places, especially in science and engineering subjects. The shortfall was partly taken up by the part-time and full-time courses offered by LEA technical colleges such as Luton College.

A HATFUL OF TALENT

Many of these courses were for Higher National Certificates rather than degrees, part-time rather than full-time attendance being required. At Luton good performance at HNC level could lead on to work towards a BSc University of London (External) degree. An alternative entry route was two A Levels in science and mathematics subjects. During this time the emphasis of the college began to change, with the science degree intake increasing at the expense of engineering degrees. Rothamsted Experimental Station at Harpenden, and Unilever at The Frythe and at Sharnbrook provided the core of part-timers. Meanwhile, a decision was taken to provide full-time courses initially fitted into the part-time teaching pattern.

The science courses in greatest demand were chemistry, botany and zoology, followed by physics and mathematics. Geology was introduced in the mid-1950s and geography in 1958. The college taught the BSc General course requiring students to take and pass at one time examinations in three subjects for Part One and two subjects for Part Two. All subjects had equal standing, except that Geography – a late comer to BSc General – had to be taken with either Chemistry or Physics. Examinations were sat in London at the Horticultural Halls and latterly at Alexandra Palace. Practical examinations were at The Imperial Institute and at the University of London Laboratories in Brunswick Square whence practical books had to be delivered. It was while travelling to these examinations that Geraint Jones, the son of a Luton police sergeant, was killed when he jumped from a burning train at Napsbury near St Albans.

The College enjoyed good results in the London BSc with about one student a year getting a first-class degree and several upper seconds. Studying two subjects to honours degree level – the finals papers in each subject were from a suite of papers taken by single-honours subject students – posed quite severe tests of candidates' abilities. It is worth noting that it was not until the late 1980s that the college moved from the combined honours degree format towards a major/minor degree and it is only in the 1990s that single-honours degrees in science have been introduced.

This slow evolution was partly because of the increasing regulation of higher education by the Ministry of Education and its successor the Department of Education & Science. Although in the 1950s permission to run higher education courses had to be sought from the Ministry, this was largely granted automatically. However, from 1963 permission to run degree-level courses had to be sought through a more complex procedure. This involved first obtaining the support of the LEA, the Regional Further Education Inspector and the Regional Advisory Committee (RAC). Luton suffered particularly, in part because it was not a polytechnic, in part because of changes in the LEA and not least because of the college's geographical location.

When the 1964 Robbins Report recommended the establishment of 34 polytechnics in England and Wales, Luton was omitted from the list. This caused great disappointment to those members of the college staff teaching to degree level, especially as Hatfield College of Technology was included. A number of letters were sent and visits made but to little avail. The reasons for lack of success only emerged much later, at least to those at teaching staff level.

The Luton catchment area – the town with a population of 153,000; the conurbation with about 200,000; and areas within one hour's travelling time with 300,000 – was the biggest population centre to be left off the list. Derby College might have argued otherwise. The geographical case for Luton in preference to Hatfield (with its much smaller catchment), Oxford, Huddersfield and Preston was put to Dr John Corbett, the Director of Education for Luton, by the Principal (Frank Stephenson) the Head of the Science Department (John Howard) and the Lecturer in Geography (David Cooper). Dr Corbett's explanation for not being able to press a case was the choice between a polytechnic and an urgent need for primary teacher training to meet the needs of the newly established county borough and of neighbouring Hertfordshire. At that time primary education took precedence, hence Putteridge Bury was established as a mature student teacher training college, independent of Luton College of Technology.

Subsequently, it transpired that when the Ministry of Education had first mooted the idea of polytechnics, Bedfordshire County Council had wanted to use Bedford's colleges as the base, at a time when these colleges had no higher education courses in science or engineering. It is also important to remember that in 1963 Luton became a County Borough with total responsibility for its education service – primary, secondary and tertiary. This did not happen overnight and effectively removed a major source of rates income from Bedfordshire. In 1973, with local government reorganisation, Luton once again became part of Bedfordshire. County council policy towards Luton College of Technology was that it should provide higher education in technology, business, management and science for the county. Nevertheless the operational relationship remained distant.

Luton lies on the edge of the London Metropolitan area and was in the North Metropolitan Higher Education region for a time. It was also in the East Anglian region for many educational functions. This location on the boundary placed the College at a disadvantage compared with "heartland" colleges and polytechnics, for example, Cambridge CAT, Hatfield and Middlesex, and continued support even for existing higher education courses often appeared to be grudgingly given by the Regional Advisory Committees.

This support had to be sought in 1972 when the college began the process of obtaining Council for National Academic Awards (CNAA) approval for science degrees. The educational climate had chilled compared with the halcyon days of the 1960s. The polytechnics had arrived and were expanding rapidly. Policy decisions regarding teacher training colleges were beginning to be made and mergers to create the colleges of higher education were beginning to be discussed. To those who were involved in writing the first CNAA submission the permission to go forward was by no means certain. Indeed permission to do so was only given after there had been a highly unofficial approach to a very important lady in government.

The local HMI frequently visited the college and he told John Howard that the application to make a change was going to be turned down. This so incensed Howard that he wrote privately to the Secretary of State for Education, Margaret Thatcher, but received a very bland reply from a civil servant. With the help of an active member of the local Conservative Party, Les Craggs, a Chemistry lecturer, a meeting was arranged with Stephen Hastings, then MP for Mid-Bedfordshire. The Principal, Roy Steed, overcame his serious misgivings about the direct approach and joined in a visit to Charles Simeons, the Luton MP, who agreed to bring the college's position to Mrs Thatcher's notice. Shortly after that, permission to submit to CNAA was received. But for this, one might conjecture, the University of Luton might never have come into being.

One aspect which has not been mentioned so far, but which is quite important, is that paralleling the full-time London external degree in sciences, with its strong part-time support, were two other University of London external degrees, the BSc (Econ) and BA (General). These usually had small followings – each course recruited 10 or so students annually, and was taught in the evenings and on Saturday mornings. While never strong these courses provided a base for degree-level teaching in the Business Studies (also known as the Commerce) Department. The courses included Economics, English, French, Geography, History and Philosophy.

Whereas a part-time student in science typically took a minimum of four years to complete his or her course, part time "evenings only" students took six years for theirs. This forward commitment frequently died with the first frosts of winter. The four-year course was two years for Part One, or one year post-HNC, then at least two years for Part Two, if the student could come full-time for all or part of the second year, if not, three years might be required.

The University of London external degree served Luton College well. From amongst the early engineering graduates several went to high places in the automotive and engineering industry; others joined Luton College as lecturers, notably Kenneth Adams and James Vass. Students from the Science course here followed distinguished research and academic careers as well as being successful in business. Rod Taylor, who was one of the first to graduate, achieved a DSc and was at one time Principal Scientific Officer in the Entomology Department at Rothamsted Experimental Station.

John Lake took a PhD and was at the National Institute of Agricultural Engineering at Silsoe; Marshal Askew was a senior research officer at ICI Laboratories, Brixham; Patrick Lewis became a chief geologist at the UN; and Mike Garrett a palaeontologist in Australia. Bob Young followed a first-class degree in Geology and Chemistry with a PhD at Imperial College, London, and runs a precious metals prospecting company. Rosemary Webb took her upper second class degree whilst working as a college technician and became a researcher for Unilever at The Frythe. Roy Outen did a similar thing and became a teacher in a local school. Bob Palmer is a surveyor with the Soil Survey. Ken Whaley did exploration geology on the Canadian Shield, as did John Parkinson, while his brother Phillip began his teaching career in Jamaica following a Geology-Geography degree. The Parkinsons' father graduated as a part-time student some years later. Kenneth Baker, who began with a GCE O Level, is managing director of a building firm. Coal and Hydrocarbons attracted a number of students with the beginning of North Sea oil development; Andrew Johnson is an international consultant; John Clure a petroleum expert and Mike Whately Lecturer in Geology in the University of Leicester, following an MSc at the University of the Witwatersrand while working in coal mining in South Africa. Rob Taylor is an exploration geologist with a major oil company.

Academic careers also attracted Hammond Murray-Ruse, who worked in Sweden, East Africa and North America; Peter Hoare who is at Anglia University teaching Soils. Ron Driver was a part-time student from Laporte before graduating and joining the Mathematics Department of Luton College to teach statistics and computing. He is now the University of Luton's Academic Registrar. Paul Heley first enrolled for an HNC in Electrical Engineering in 1955 before progressing to a BSc in Mathematics and Geology while teaching at the College in 1970, followed by an MSc in Mathematical Geology; John Plater took his degree in Chemistry and Mathematics, also as a part-time student, before joining the teaching staff. Pat Fry similarly joined the Biology staff. Audrey Garner was one of the earlier graduates who has returned to the university technical staff.

Some Luton graduates from this period have followed careers quite removed from front-line science work. Cathy Johnson runs a craft centre and Willy Henderson is a Housing Officer in Oxfordshire.

Teaching the London external degree course was a challenge. Although the university published regulations, its syllabuses were remarkably vague, or in some cases non-existent. Geology was taught against past examination papers. The university's advice was "to teach the subject and forget the examination". To have some idea of what might appear on the question paper, close liaison was maintained with University of London teaching departments, for example, Norman D' Cruz at University College. He, Peter Keay and Albert Ludford eventually became examiners, which provided a little more insight. The goodwill built up at that time between Luton and London has continued, as has the academic relationship with other universities, notably Cambridge and Oxford. Even so, most candidates went to their examinations aware that the examiner's pet subject might be one that their lecturers regarded as of marginal importance.

The first Head of the Science Department at Luton College of Technology, Miss Nora Boothman, took the view that potentially every student who successfully completed a GCE O Level or City and Guilds course in her department could take a degree. She interviewed all full-time students and many part-time students during the Spring Term of each year and told them so too. After Miss Boothman retired in December 1964, her successor, John Howard, maintained the practice and then passed the task to the section leaders in the major subjects to continue.

Students would arrive from the local secondary modern schools to attempt GCE O Level in one year. Officially we only had permission to run one-year repeat A Level courses for sixth form failures but they could always be taken twice! A Level GCE courses were a major source of recruiting from the local grammar schools and the private schools in the adjacent counties. Students achieved their A Levels and the highest achievers usually left for a university, but a substantial number continued at Luton to "The Degree". Among the "all through" students were John Clure, Stuart Hollyer, who is now with the British Geological Survey at Keyworth, and Sandra Keeller.

The necessity of passing three subjects at one go at Part One in the London external degree made it a very substantial challenge and naturally a number of students failed. These were not lost to the college but became basic-grade technicians there, in local schools or, later, at Barnfield College or at Rothamsted Experimental Station. Having passed Part One as part-timers, students usually began their Part Two course as part-timers, returning to full-time study in the "third year". Alan Hill, BSc Geography and Geology, who found Physics a problem, but who is a town planner in Luton, was an example of this practice.

The need for the safety net became less pressing when the University of London reduced the number of subjects in Part One from three to two. Its operation became more cumbersome as employment in the college was restricted by greater financial stringency, although technicians were and are still encouraged to take degree courses.

A small but significant number of students took postgraduate professional qualifications in sciences offered at the college. Courses ran through the 1960s and 1970s for Membership of the Institute of Biology and for Graduate of the Royal Institute of Chemistry.

A significant development in the late 1960s was the establishment of college research studentships. These were initially only one a year. Chris Taylor, Bill Maguire and Pete Richards are examples of students who achieved doctorates at the University of London partly supported by these studentships, which laid the foundation for a base of research teaching essential to any future university.

Another activity which supported high-quality teaching was the institution of a series of symposia. First suggested by employers of part-time students, notably Unilever, these attracted international audiences. The first one, "Enzymes" was chaired by Professor Ernest Gale, Head of Biochemistry at Cambridge University. Professor Ian Marton, who for some years was a member of the College Governing Body, took an active part in the selection of topics. Linked to this was staff research, with advisers coming from Rothamsted Experimental Station and other research institutes. Their task was to ensure quality, as the annual interview with Dr John Burgoyne, or Dr Penman, FRS, was not an easy one. Among those who successfully completed research degrees were John Harding (PhD Zoology), Albert Ludford (PhD Geology), R A Baker (MSc Zoology), Edward Eastwood (MSc Zoology), Ron Beard (MSc Education) and Paul Heley (MSc Geology)

To serve both college and local needs, programmes of invitation lectures were offered with titles like "Progression of Geography". Speakers under this heading ranged from Richard Chorley, a geomorphologist at Cambridge University, to John Hunt and Eric Shipton, mountaineers and explorers.

The early CNAA years

As the polytechnics emerged, the government developed a new degree awarding body to cater for them, the Council for National Academic Awards (CNAA). The University of London had found difficulty in coping with the massive expansion in external student numbers in the late 1960s, particularly in arts subjects. The pressure was greatest on examiners because the university would not appoint non-University of London graduates to that role. In 1970 it announced that from 1973 onwards it would cease to register full-time students in other institutions for its external degrees.

In 1967 as CNAA was first coming into existence, Dr Fred Webber, then Principal Lecturer in Botany at Luton College, had led a small group of staff who had looked into the possibility of transferring from the London external degree. This move came to nothing, since the college preferred to stay with the University of London, and Dr Webber left to become Head of the Department of Botany at Wolverhampton Polytechnic. One reason for not transferring was that the external London degrees were seen as having greater prestige than the then unknown CNAA degrees. This notion was quickly dispelled as the CNAA introduced the rigour of peer assessment into its validation processes. It also proved a mistake not to be in at the beginning of the CNAA's development, necessitating a slow and frequently painful adjustment process later. (One nickname given to the CNAA was Council for Nasty Amounts of Aggro.)

A HATFUL OF TALENT

The process of preparing the first submission of a degree course to the CNAA offers an interesting insight into course administration and college management at a time of rapid change. The early 1970s was the period when expansion was replaced by extending the democratisation of college organisation. This was the time when Academic Boards at college and departmental level came into existence and staff were given opportunity to elect their representatives to those bodies, although the majority membership remained *de jure* or *ex-officio*.

Following the initial submission of a request to change our science degree course from the University of London to the CNAA made via the college governors to the LEA and the Regional Advisory Council, help was sought from CNAA on the format of the submission. This involved no more than a meeting with officers at the CNAA office in Devonshire Place, London. The main body of the work was done as an iterative process by a committee formed of the two heads of department, Henry Horner for Mathematics and John Howard for Science, and the subject leaders.

It was felt that the job of the course leader should be given to someone with experience of CNAA committee work. David Cooper had been invited to join the first geography subject panel by its chairman, Professor Stanley H Beaver of the University of Keele. He was the only Luton College lecturer on a CNAA committee until 1976.

Dr Albert Ludford joined the Geology panel in 1976. Cooper's membership of the committee only lasted three years, as the peer groups from polytechnics and colleges with approved courses grew, and entailed only three validation visits to Portsmouth, Middlesex and Ealing. Despite his comparative inexperience he became responsible for the first submission.

Knowing something of the demands which the CNAA was placing upon institutions to ensure that its degrees were of equivalent standard to degrees awarded by universities, Cooper embarked on a preliminary document outlining to the college management what would be expected by way of facilities, equipment and teaching resources. This was accepted, but the message came back that the resources would have to be earned as no special capital allocations could be made. Equipment and facilities were to become the key issues dogging the validation processes of the college's submissions for the next 15 years.

The Science Department staff were not helped by being seen by the rest of the college as the favoured few, a specialised group of staff teaching a small number of students with a high demand on the college budget. This was strongly challenged by the science staff at every opportunity pointing to their supporting work in A Levels, ONC, HNC, HND and similar courses.

The committee given the task of writing the submission comprised the two heads of department (Henry Horner and John Howard), Les Craggs

(Chemistry), Bill Roe (Physics), Albert Ludford (Geology), Neil Sealey (Geography), Ron Driver (Mathematics), Garth Fish (Mathematics), David Orwin (Environmental Biology) and Peter Keay (Cell Biology).

Secretarial support was given by Lynne Butler, who at that time worked in the general office where the University Registry is presently located. Meetings were held at all sorts of times during the working day to fit in with teaching and cause least disruption to it. Evenings were the time for writing and rewriting. One feature which markedly differed from present practice was to read the documents aloud to ensure good grammar and syntax.

In designing the course, it was decided that for the first period of approval the subjects would be basically those hitherto taught for the BSc London degree and offering a similar pattern of third-year options which would form the honours components. Students would take two subjects of equal status, certain combinations not being permitted, for example Geography and Cell Biology. There was relatively little emphasis on study skills, computing still being in infancy, but there was some mathematics in all courses at Part One.

The Part One course took one year; Part Two, two years with no examination at the end of the first of these. THE CNAA was reluctant to accept this form and it was probably the least popular feature of the course with students who felt they had no yardstick on progress. Each of the subject leaders chaired a subject committee which debated the content and format of this proposed syllabus. These groups tended to meet at lunch times and in the twilight break between the afternoon and evening sessions. While the basic structure of the degree and the major subjects remained those of the London degree, some contact changes were made to come into line with staff interest and expertise.

As now, the final days before the sending off the submission were hectic. The Principal's Secretary, Pam Vachon, joined Lynne Butler in typing the Gestetner skins, with other office staff running off the pages. The covers were printed at the Luton Town Hall press and the volume bound in college. One subject almost missed the final deadline for submission. The document was sent to the CNAA shortly after approval had been received from the Regional Staff Inspector on behalf of the Advisory Committee for the course to move to CNAA.

The validation meeting with the CNAA's panel was for most the first experience of the confrontational approach which characterised Luton College's early experience of the CNAA. Dr Maurice Foss chaired for the CNAA and subjects had their own visiting panel member or members. The main meeting was in the old committee room on the first floor where the Vice Chancellor's suite now is. Substantial changes were required of each subject. Severe criticism was made of the level of equipment and it was laid down that mathematics was not to be taught beyond part one level without major change. The first objective had been achieved, and students could be enrolled on the CNAA degree course. However, the 1973 Science degree enrolment proved to be disappointingly small compared with the previous London years. Thirteen students had their degrees conferred on 30 October 1976, Kevin Myers achieving a first-class honours. There were two upper seconds, two lower seconds, five thirds, and three ordinary degrees, probably not a lot worse than in later external degree times. Conferment was by Professor Philip Graham, Professor of Child Psychiatry in the University of London, whose father had a dental practice on the Park Square site and who had taken his GCE A Levels at the college to qualify for Cambridge University.

The Staff Asssociation Annual Dinner . . . and Dance, 1965

BILL AITKEN

JUST BEFORE I started work at Luton College as an assistant lecturer, David Cooper, the secretary of the Staff Association, wrote inviting me to make up a party for the association's Annual Dinner and Dance to be held on 2 January 1965. The event was being held at the George Hotel, Luton, then the town's major venue for social events. Dress was formal, dinner suits for men and long dresses for ladies, and tickets were one guinea (£1.05 – to put this in perspective, the average lecturer's salary was then about £1,000).

The ballroom was set out for dinner when we arrived and the crowd was thronging the adjacent cocktail bar. The top table was arranged along the length of the room to accommodate the large number of VIPs, something which was to have a decided effect on the evening's proceedings. My wife and I with two friends found our seats on one of the sprigs leading off the top table and we noticed that several of the diners near us were wearing their chains of office. They were obviously official guests who could not be accommodated on the top table. The top table itself contained a fair sprinkling of mayoral chains and I observed our local MP, Will Howie (now Lord Howie of Troon), sitting at the far end.

Luton was a County Borough in those days and Luton College was the only college between Bedford and Watford, so it drew on a huge catchment area. Frank Stephenson, the Principal, was extremely good at public relations and had invited almost every influential council member for miles around. Frank was a genial fellow and one of the old style principals who actually enjoyed a drink with the staff in the local pubs. I did not realise at the time that Staff Association events were one of Frank's vehicles for oiling the wheels of further education in Luton, an essential activity in those times when continuity and growth in FE depended so much on local authority initiative.

A HATFUL OF TALENT

After dinner we settled back with our cigarettes and cigars – almost everybody smoked in those days – to listen to the Principal's address and perhaps – we anticipated – a reply from an honoured guest. Frank spoke first and recounted the great successes of the college during the previous year, with a little bit tacked on from previous years. He also castigated some owners of land in the Vicarage Street area, who had showed lack of public spiritedness by appealing against compulsory purchase orders on their property. The resulting appeals procedure had held up the building of a new junior feeder college adjacent to Park Square. My guests were suitably impressed that I was joining a prestigious organisation and we nodded at the mention of each achievement and gave Frank a well-deserved round of applause at the end of his speech.

The Mayor was the next speaker. He proceeded to give us a serious appraisal of the College and Luton's pride in its achievement. Frank, who was now acting as master of ceremonies, replied to the Mayor's comments at some length and then, to our horror, introduced the Chairman of the Education Committee, who was a stalwart supporter and necessary ally of the college. My guests, who had come for a dinner and dance, now looked at me in dismay at the prospect of another earnest entreaty on civic pride and the value of education.

But worse was to come. Other speakers were invited to say a few words, each accompanied by a reply from the Principal. This situation was exacerbated by the fact that the Head of the Department of Science, Miss Nora Boothman, was retiring after many years and this evening was also being used to present her with her a parting gift. And of course this entailed two further speeches – a valedictory one from Frank and a reply from Miss Boothman. She had given sterling service to the Institution and was well deserving of the accolade and entitled to a reply. Her reply did contain the only humorous content of the evening so far but I noticed that even so one of my guests had dozed off. The band hired for the evening could be heard laughing through the glass doors of the cocktail bar.

At approximately 11.10pm a loud derisive cheer went up from the captive audience when the Principal announced that the speeches were over. The cheer was not surprising considering that the evening had started at 7.15pm. But our relief was short-lived, for a commotion arose from the right hand of the top table from Will Howie. The Principal was mistaken, the speeches were not over, Will had also been invited to add his contribution to the evening and was not going to forfeit this opportunity. Even at this late hour, he gave us another 25 minutes of discourse on architecture, education and the Ministry of Works. Fascinating stuff it may have been, but to a speech-weary audience, at that time of night, it was far from riveting. My friends gave me a look of

36

disbelief and reminded me not to invite them again the next year.

Eventually the speeches were over. The tables still had to be cleared for dancing but the Band returned from the bar and the audience was allowed to make an overdue visit to the toilets. It was now 11.40pm and the evening finished at about 12.45am.

Somebody had decided that we should start with a barn dance which was to be led by Jim Vass, one of my future colleagues from the Engineering department. By the time we got through that there was just time for a couple of dances before the last waltz.

Our party went to a friend's house for coffee before going home and by now we were hysterical with disbelief at the sequence of events. I did at least feel secure in the knowledge that if local and junior parliamentary politics had any real power then the Luton College had a healthy future.

I have told this story many times in the college bar and over the years it may have become slightly exaggerated, but I can testify to its general accuracy. Ask anybody who was there and managed to stay awake for the whole evening.

Postscript: *The Staff Association did survive for another 28 years, throughout the various developments of the college, providing a range of social activities for the staff. Unfortunately it has not survived in the larger institution of the university.* ■

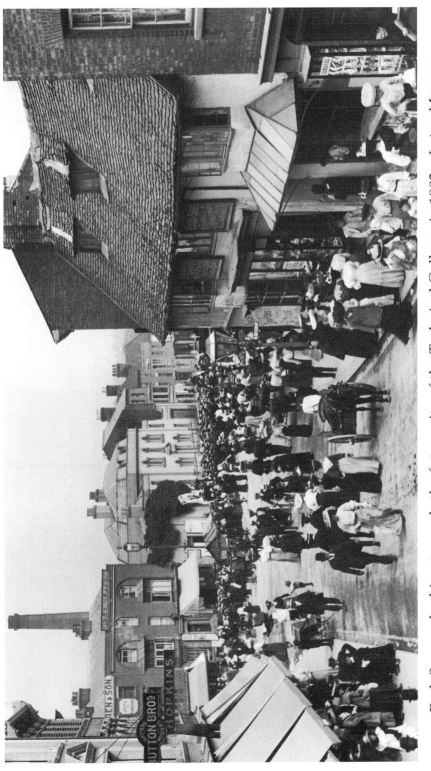

Park Square, looking towards the future site of the Technical College, in 1902 – *Luton Museum*

The White House, family home built for the Burr family whose brewery stood alongside – *Luton Museum*

Park Square c.1910. The Modern/Technical School stands on the right on the site of the White House, demolished c.1908. On the left can be seen the sign of The Cock public house – *Luton Museum/Eric Meadows*

Luton Modern School c.1908. The establishment had previously been using buildings on the other side of Park Square

TAE Sanderson and staff of Luton Modern School, 1908. Sanderson's clear prejudice in favour of science did not please all within the town who felt that the wider aspects of education were being neglected. To him, however, should go credit for initially developing technical and further education to meet some of the needs of the new engineering firms which were recruiting and training within Luton – *Luton Museum*

Luton Modern School girls exercising in the yard at the rear of the school in 1908 – *Luton Museum*

One example of College Principal WF Stephenson's determination to integrate college and industry during the 1950s and 1960s – an industrial "Brains Trust" hosted by the Technical College at which Stephenson and representatives of local firms fielded questions from a predominantly student audience. Hundreds of students would queue during enrolment for places on the College's courses.

The intensely vocational nature of the Technical College's courses included this 1953 class on window dressing display which was attended by no fewer than 80 pupils. Here the tutor, K A Thresh, gives advice to Patricia Cox on displaying cake icing accessories – *Luton Museum*

Luton's Chief Education Officer, Dr Corbett, awarding a prize to a distinctly underwhelmed school pupil in the early 1950s. The dominant figure in the town's educational development during the 1950s and 1960s, Corbett combined a deceptively relaxed managerial style with the disarming ability to give the impression that he knew each of the town's teaching staff by name– *Luton Museum*

A moment of personal satisfaction, as well as civic pride, for John Burgoyne and Hedley Lawrence (on the right in the Mayoral chain) at the foundation stone-laying ceremony for the new college on 4 May 1955

Luton Museum

Aerial photograph of the new college in 1957

John Burgoyne being enrolled as the 5,000th student in January 1954, to study "Methods Engineering". With him are (left to right) JH Jeffs (Registrar), DG Lintern (Head of Department of Commerce and Administration) and JH Knowles (Assistant Registrar). Burgoyne's enrolment was not merely a publicity gimmick, he also retained a love for the virtues of education throughout his life – *Luton Museum*

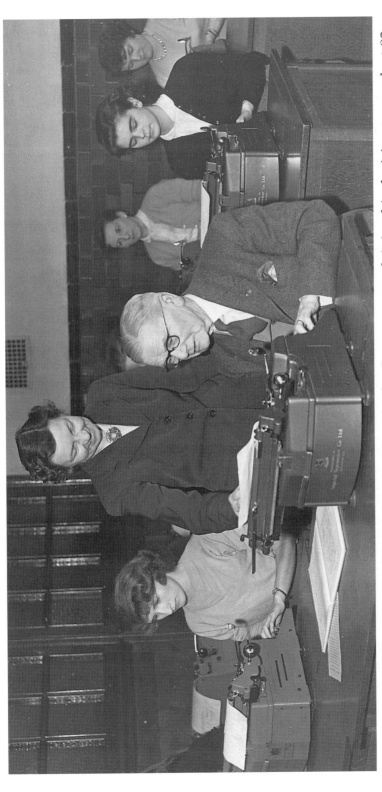

"It's easier to tap out letters than write them," said John Burgoyne, explaining his decision to enrol, at 82, in a typing class in January 1958 as student no. 7,000. With the new College nearing completion, Burgoyne added: "Here I see convincing evidence that this college is fully answering the purpose for which it has been provided." – *Luton Museum*

An attentive audience listens to the speeches at the formal opening of the College in June 1960. For many years the College's hall played host to a variety of concerts, exhibitions and performances in a town largely bereft of suitable venues – *Luton Museum*

An exhibition hosted by the College in June 1963, and by Luton's clothing industry, in order to promote the trade. Overshadowed by engineering, the local clothing firms were struggling to recruit skilled labour and targeted the event at schools in an attempt to entice leavers – *Luton Museum*

Students 'hoof it' across the stage at a College Review c.1960. The provision of a building to match the number of students encouraged an expansion of events and amenities. These included a College Sailing Club at Tiddenfoot Quarry, near Linslade – *Luton Museum*

The Student Union Executive Committee in October 1963. For the first time there was a concerted attempt to improve female students' representation. "At first, the boys took it all as a joke. Then they saw that we were serious and their attitude to the elections changed completely," said Jennifer Ridings, the new Secretary. Until this time apathy had characterised participation in the Student Union. From left to right: Alan Jones, David Ward, Diane Barras-Smith, John Allsop, Jennifer Ridings, Tony Tuck and Michael Graves-Morris. There were a further four girls elected to the twelve-strong Council – *Luton Museum*

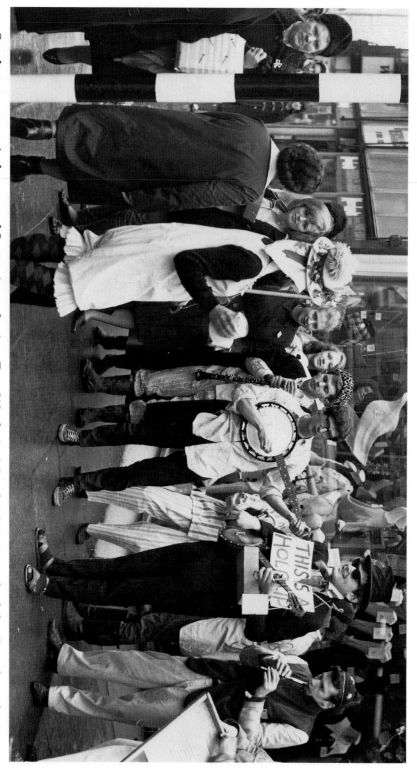

Students entertain bemused Lutonians during Rag Week, in March 1964, in aid of the Freedom from Hunger Campaign – *Luton Museum*

Archery practice in the gymnasium c.1970

Opening of the new Computer Centre in April 1985. From left to right: Dr Tony Wood, J Marshall, Graham Bright MP, Nicholas Phillips (Deputy Lieutenant of Bedfordshire) and Lucy Phillips

The leader of the opposition, the Rt. Hon Neil Kinnock MP, is welcomed to the College by the Director during a visit in 1987. In the centre is Mrs Pam Vachon.

Lord Prior is presented with a memento following the opening of the Company Suite at Putteridge Bury on 20 April 1988 – *Mike Pierce*

Herald   Thursday, May 12, 1988

'Act now — or create an educational desert'

COLLEGE PLA[N] SPARKS FUR[Y]

FURIOUS councillors have called an emergency meeting to try to block an "illegal" college move to opt out of the county education system.

The governors of Luton College have acted outside the law, accused Labour and Democrats at last Thursday's annual county council meeting.

By MIKE GLACKEN

The row broke out when it was revealed the college board voted to notify the Education Secretary they intend to apply to join the new Polytechnics and Colleges Funding Council.

The governors are ~~supported~~ by lecturers ~~as well as~~

college to carry out this intention, which is a matter for the county council to decide.

"A junior minister has been asking colleges to act outside the law when it has been made clear they have no right to do so," accused Labour leader Councillor John Tizard.

~~governors went~~ ~~the legal~~

college."

But unrepentant Councillor Lester told the meeting: "I don't give a tuppeny damn for these criticisms. Councillors appointed as governors are there to act in the best interests of the governing bodies."

The Labour and Democratic majority voted to support the status quo in higher ~~education~~, and demand ~~retraction~~

[FUTURE of higher educa]tion [to] be bleak if Luton Colle[ge]

's the grim warning from di[rector] g directly for public suppor[t]

[to ha]ve higher [status] free itself [from c]ontrol of [Count]y Coun-[cil]

[school aims stu]-[dents'] busi-[ness] unless [with] [futu]res of [and to] the [contr]olled Col-

economic and effects on Luton South Bedford could be consider with the long- continuation of co for 3,000 local stud from industry and ness being in doubt annual injection of million into the econ being threatened. the range of tech

Report by MIKE GLACKE[N]

Student power behind chief

LUTON College director Dr Tony Wood was defended by students when he came under fire for the college's bid to join the elite Polytechnics and Colleges Funding Council.

A move to condemn his "unprofessional insubordination" for refusing to stick to county council policy was tabled at Monday's meeting of the further education sub-committee.

But earlier the students' union contacted the Herald with a statement supporting their principal and objecting to an "unwarranted attack" on an officer of the college.

Criticisms

"In our opinion the director has acted quite correctly and is within the mandate given him by the governing body, to whom any criticisms should be properly addressed," says their statement.

The issue was raised by the Government's education reform bill, they say, and the governors were given all relevant information, including the county secretary's opinion that they had no legal right to act without council backing.

Students' union administrator Robin Yates, who is also a governor, added: "It is hitting below the belt to criticse an officer. The county council had bags of time to support or oppose this if they wished. If this move is not made it will leave Bedfordshire in an educational desert."

College wins fight for independence

LUTON College has won its battle for independence — and will now join the ranks of other top educational institutions throughout Britain.

Instead of being run by Beds County Council, the college is to be funded nationally. The result could be more prestige for the college in the future, and greater opportunities for different types of courses for local students and those from other parts of the country.

Luton South MP Graham Bright (Con) has worked flat out to get the college funded by the Polytechnics and Colleges Funding Council. He has just heard that the college has had its application accepted.

Said Mr Bright, who lobbied Ministers constantly on behalf of the college: "I am absolutely delighted that we have won. The director, governors and staff put an excellent case.

"The college offers excellent higher education and vocational courses, management and technical training. It will now be free to develop them still further as a national institution."

He criticised Beds County Council, which tried to stop the college joining the PCFC. He slammed some of the councillors who opposed the college's bid, and called them "backwoodsmen".

College director Dr Tony Wood said: "The move means the potential for a wider range of higher education courses at the college, and more opportunity for study for the people and industry of Bedfordshire."

He thanked the three local MPs who had backed the struggle by the college, and also praised local business people who had done everything possible to make sure the Luton College got membership of the PCFC.

The college students' union has given a guarded welcome that the college was to be included in the PCFC. Steve Duff, president of the union, said the future of higher education was not safe in the hands of the Government, but the short-term interests of students were best served through the PCFC.

Beds County Council said it was "greatly concerned and disappointed" at the Government's decision to let Luton College opt out of local authority control.

A statement from the council said it was now concerned for the future not only of Luton College but three other colleges in the county.

Beds County Council Labour group said the Government had demonstrated "contempt for elected education authorities". It warned of Luton College: "Under the PCFC arrangements its future will be bleak. It could well become a subsidiary of Hatfield Polytechnic. It could be closed in less than ten years."

Newspaper cuttings

*Just some of the vegetarian specialities we have
on offer, but not all on the same day!*

Spinach & cream cheese canneloni

Vegetable lasagne

Samosas

Vegetable tikka masala

Vegetarian chilli

Cauliflower cheese

Leek mornay

Mushroom crepes

Macaroni cheese

Vegeburgers

Wholemeal vegetable pasties

Jacket potatoes with cheese/coleslaw

Cheese & onion pasties

'Healthy Eating' Salads

Courgette & tomato

Spicy pasta

Waldorf

Beansprout

Mixed bean

Coleslaw

Rice

Mixed green

Striped Boater menu

Putteridge Bury

Based on information provided by
VAL DEMPSEY & FIONA HOWARTH

IN THE EARLY 1960s class sizes in many primary schools in the larger industrial towns and cities increased dramatically because of teacher shortages. Within the schools were teachers who were highly motivated and experienced but unqualified. Historically, unqualified status within the profession has been an unacceptable method of solving a teacher shortage. Mature students were seen to be the national answer to the problem. While the population was at the time reasonably mobile, mature trainee teachers trained in their own localities was a solution that answered a number of logistic problems. Small, local colleges dedicated to teacher training could provide for day students; two-year courses for those with appropriate experience and/or equivalent entry qualifications would be provided; and there would be opportunities for "retreads" – mature students who wished to change direction completely. This included a concept which was unusual at this time: opportunities for highly qualified former members of the armed forces to transfer their skills to the sciences, thus bringing real experience into schools. Dedicated courses were written and validated by the relevant area training organisations, usually the institute of education of the nearest university.

Luton Education Authority recognised that a local non-residential college would go a long way towards solving its own teacher shortages, and late in 1964 advertised locally and in neighbouring areas to establish the number of mature students likely to take up such an opportunity. This suggested the possibility of an intake of up to 80 students a year (including an intake from north Hertfordshire). Luton then approached Hertfordshire County Council with the suggestion that Putteridge Bury, a country house in Hertfordshire some two miles from the centre of Luton, should be converted to provide training for up to 300 students travelling daily from lodgings or their homes in Luton, other parts of Bedfordshire and north Hertfordshire.

Hertfordshire County Council agreed to the proposal and in 1965

A HATFUL OF TALENT

Putteridge Bury was sold to Luton Borough Council which began converting it. Later the same year advertisements appeared in the *Times Educational Supplement* for staff for Putteridge Bury College of Education, which was to be opened from 1 April 1966 with a further intake to follow in September 1966. Dr J. H. Corbett, Luton's Chief Education Officer, was charged with the task of creating the provision at Putteridge Bury, which had been last used as research laboratories by British Celanese. Dr Corbett had great qualities, including his apparent ability to name all his teachers and have a personal interest in their development. George Humphries, BSC, DFC, a former Pathfinder, Headteacher, Local Authority Inspector and Principal of a teacher training college in Nigeria, was appointed as Principal, and Miss Betty Rollings and Mrs M. Tassell were transferred from the Education Office to provide the administrative machinery. Mr Ron Swallow, a Headteacher at Maidenhall Primary School for many years, was to create the bridge between the schools and the college. It was he who would help with organising teaching practice in local schools. His vast experience was to be invaluable to the growth of the college.

Early appointments were of the staff required to ensure that quality courses would begin from the appointed day. Rarely is the opportunity available to start from scratch with a carefully chosen staff. The strength of the team lay in its balance of recent teaching experience in primary schools with teacher training experience in the various age ranges. Quite rightly very talented staff were drawn from the borough. James Dyer, FSA, an archaeologist with a national reputation, was teaching primary school children at Stopsley. Molly Stebbings and Alfreda Lewis were to bring their art and music skills from the former Luton Girls' High School. Horace Bradding, a Cambridge mathematician, was to come straight from school along with geographer Roy Gore. John Holborrow was to head the Art Group. Alan Flint was highly successful in making science relevant. The Education Team was led by Gill Briggs who along with Brenda Dennis (English) came with vast experience of teacher training. Val Dempsey, who was to become Vice-Principal two years later, was appointed from Wolverhampton Teachers' College. From the outset the staff : student ratio was established at 1 : 10 and George Humphries appointed people who not only demonstrated a knowledge of their subject but also enthusiasm and commitment.

After appointments were made, letters, lists and syllabuses flew to and fro. Meetings were held with principles and priorities being established. The normal qualifications for entry to teacher training was five GCE O levels, but all applicants were interviewed. Where candidates lacked these qualifications but looked likely to be suitable, they were offered the opportunity to be interviewed by the Director of the Cambridge Institute of Education for admission in a "special entry" category.

40

Putteridge Bury: a brief recent history

The present house at Putteridge Bury, an estate that dates back to Domesday Book and beyond, was built between 1908 and 1911 for the brewer Thomas Clutterbuck, whose family sold it to Sir Felix Cassel in 1928. During the Second World War the house was requisitioned by the government for use by the armed forces – later in the war, prisoners of war were housed in Nissen huts in the grounds. After the death of Sir Felix in 1953, the house was sold to the textiles company British Celanese which converted it for use as research laboratories.

In 1965 the house was acquired by Luton Borough Council and in 1966 Putteridge Bury College of Education was opened. When the college merged with Luton College in 1978, the Department of Business and Management Studies, which was outgrowing its facilities at Park Square, took over the building, sharing it for a while with Luton Sixth Form College. The Management Centre flourished at its new site in the 1980s, with student numbers peaking at 800.

With the arrival of Dr Tony Wood as Director of Luton College in 1985, Putteridge Bury took on a new role, as the Centre for Applied Technology and Innovation (CATI), which was intended to be a highly entrepreneurial centre providing a natural focus for business activity. Realising the potential of the house, Dr Wood set about restoring the function rooms to their original splendour and converting the unused gymnasium to a practical learning resources centre with closed-circuit TV and viewing room. The old kitchens were converted to laboratories to service applied research contracts and the house's original main reception rooms were renovated to conference centre standards.

In December 1987, Fiona Howarth joined as General Manager, taking over the development of the Conference Centre and full-cost training courses. An unusual innovation of CATI was a mobile training and exhibition centre in a Flexibus. This was equipped with Epson computers and was capable of providing a fully independent training location anywhere in the UK. Training was delivered in locations ranging from London to Scotland, and included contracts for British Telecom to provide awareness training for 1,500 of its personnel on its new computerised customer service system and a 13-week recruitment drive for Britannia Airways.

Between 1990 and 1993 the Conference and Management Centres were amalgamated and the Research Centre moved to the John Matthews Centre.

Putteridge Bury played an important role in the celebration of the designation of the University of Luton in July 1993 when a garden party and celebration dinner was held there.

A HATFUL OF TALENT

The working and learning environment at Putteridge Bury was idyllic. The building and grounds required considerable refurbishment but George Humphries resisted the temptation to divert resources on the beautifying of the building, preferring to prioritise spending on enhancing teacher training. This meant that most problems at Putteridge Bury were of the domestic variety, such as the problem of transporting food from the Edwardian kitchens to the canteen some distance away, negotiating trollies up and down steps. The grounds, with rose garden, box hedges and vast expanses of lawn, contrasted dramatically with other local places of learning. The atmosphere at the college in the early years was a heady one as the infectious enthusiasm of students and new staff worked to the benefit of all. Music became a feature of college life, through the teachers which it produced and the concerts which were arranged. Family days were organised in order that those related to the students could share in the life of Putteridge Bury and understand more of what went on there.

Putteridge Bury was formally administered by Luton County Borough (until local government reorganisation in 1974) but the Governing Body included members from Hertfordshire. Among them was Lady Bowes Lyon, and members of the Hertfordshire County Council Education Office. This was an invaluable injection of experience from which all parties could only benefit as at that time Hertfordshire was at the forefront of education thinking and provision. (Furthermore, it had considerable "political clout", which attracted attention locally when, much to Luton's disappointment, Hatfield College was granted polytechnic status.)

George Humphreys enjoyed the close support of Dr Corbett, but the retirement of the latter, followed by Luton's loss of county borough status in 1974 and the consequent transfer of the education authority to Bedford, inevitably made the relationship with the local authority more distant. The perceived diversion of commitment and resources towards colleges in Bedford diminished staff morale, as did the national shift in emphasis away from the teacher training in which Putteridge Bury had specialised. What had hitherto been regarded as a reliable career now ceased to be so and it was within the context of survival that the merger with Luton College of Higher Education, an institution with which Putteridge Bury had very little contact in the first 10 years of its existence, has to be appreciated. The initiative for merger came from the colleges concerned rather than the education authority and throughout it all Dr Roy Steed, the Principal of Luton College, behaved with gentlemanly tact. When merger occurred in 1978 the staff at Putteridge Bury were dispersed between Luton, colleges in Bedford or took early retirement. The later history of Putteridge Bury's role in the development of Luton College and the University of Luton is described briefly in the box on page 41.

Luton College 1967–84: An Overview

ROY STEED

I WAS ONCE introduced on a public occasion as Director of the College in Park Square, "whatever its name is now"!

My appointment from September 1967 was to the Principalship of the then Luton College of Technology. My predecessor had done an excellent job. He had established the college as a large further education institution and had seen it housed in fine purpose-built premises at Park Square. The college – affectionately known as The Tec – had some 15 per cent of its total work classified as higher education and a total full-time staff of around 300.

In the next 17 years (and one term – I always said I would retire at Christmas!) the college was gradually transformed. On the way, the college acquired, towards the end of the 1970s, the elegant country mansion and grounds of Putteridge Bury and an excellent purpose-built hall of residence, one of only a few built in those years for colleges other than polytechnics; degree courses in physical, biological and earth sciences were updated and validated by the Council for National Academic Awards in place of courses for external degree examinations of the University of London, and additional Higher National Diploma and Certificate courses were accredited by the new Business and Technician Education Council; the college became largely autonomous, the Director, in association with the Academic Board, appointing all staff under arrangement agreed by the Governing Body; many further education courses were transferred to the two local further education institutions – Barnfield College and Dunstable College – and in 1978 the college was designated a College of Higher Education with a Director instead of a Principal.

By 1984, just over half the work of the college was classified as higher education, with a substantial part of the rest being in the grey area between further and higher education, and the total full-time staff (teaching and non-teaching) had grown to 450. It became the largest college by volume of both total and higher education work from Hatfield to Leicester, from Oxford to the Wash! It continued to be held in high regard and became known, locally and nationally, as Luton College.

The college always had three major objectives; first, and principally, to be a first-class teaching institution; second, to be a united community, teaching staff, non-teaching staff and students; third, to serve those concerns, industrial, commercial and public, wherever they might be, which provided employment for students of the college, either while they were at the college or when they had qualified. In general, the college always satisfied these aspirations and long may this continue in Luton, whatever the name of the institution.

To finish this brief overview with a personal reflection, Luton College has completed my "tapestry". All six educational establishments in which I served were, or have become, universities! Thank you – and goodbye – Luton College. Welcome the University of Luton, perhaps the name changing is now really over. ■

Eric's System Pays Off

JESSIE MANLEY

IN 1972 ERIC ASHTON, a principal lecturer in the Management and Professional Studies Department, became the toast of the college as far as 35 members of staff were concerned.

They belonged to the college's unofficial football pools syndicate and they had learned, to their delight, that the system devised by Eric had "come up" to the tune of £67,000. That represented a great deal of money in 1972, for it was long before the days of one and two million pound payouts.

Most of the syndicate found themselves £1,300 better off for their outlay of 20p. Others were even more fortunate as they had "invested" 40p a week and so were eligible for two shares.

The win created great excitement and made headlines in the local paper. A Littlewoods representative visited the college to present the cheque and there was much enjoyable discussion on the best ways to spend the windfall. Foreign holidays suddenly became particularly popular, the college car park saw an influx of new models (a Vauxhall family saloon cost £1,317 in those days) and other members plumped for home improvements.

A not unexpected sequel to the story was an unprecedented demand to join the syndicate. "Before the win it was sometimes difficult to drag 20p out of the members each week," said Jessie Manley, the volunteer cash collector, "but afterwards, for a few weeks at least, it became very easy!"

However, there were no more big wins in the pipeline. The most the syndicate won again was £300 and that was "reinvested" – alas without any further financial success.

Hopes, and interest, gradually evaporated and, like the syndicate, eventually faded away completely. But it was great fun while it lasted. ∎

One Brick Upon Another

BOB OXTOBY

> To put one brick upon another,
> Add a third and then a fourth,
> Leaves no time to wonder whether
> What you do has any worth.
> Philip Larkin*

IN 1994 I COMPLETED my 30th year of employment in education. I have rarely stopped to ask myself whether what I was doing had any worth; and I don't intend to start now. But my relatively short spell at Luton College of Higher Education (June 1980 to October 1984)) was certainly important for me personally and, with hindsight, I think it can be said that the early 1980s were critical years for the college as well.

At the time of my appointment as Deputy Director, the further particulars for the post carried a warning that during the next few years "it was very unlikely that there will be any significant increase in the resources presently available to the College". I have learnt to be suspicious about predictions affecting the future of higher education, but in this case, the prediction turned out to be totally accurate.

When I applied for my current job I was able to claim that I had worked in a wide variety of institutions – universities, colleges of education, colleges of technology, polytechnics, colleges of higher education. How times have changed. All these institutions are now universities (Leeds, Essex, Portsmouth, Huddersfield, Greenwich, Luton) and, although I have clear memories of each of them, these memories are clouded by events not directly related to the institution and its development. So when I think of Luton, I think not only about higher education and the college, but also about the town, its shops and its

---

* "To Put One Brick Upon Another" is from Philip Larkin, *Collected Poems*, ed. Anthony Thwaite (Faber & Faber, 1988), reproduced by kind permission of the Trustees of the Estate of Philip Larkin

football team, about Letchworth (where I lived), my children and their schooling, about trips to Cambridge and to London, holidays in Italy, Spain and the Yorkshire Dales, and about happenings on the world stage – invasion of the Falkland Islands, the election of Ronald Reagan, the marriage of Charles and Diana, the formation of the SDP, John Lennon's death, and Geoff Boycott becoming the most prolific run-scorer in Test cricket history.

Further and higher education operated within a much more restrictive organisational framework 10 to 15 years ago than is the case today. Decision-making was protracted, committee-dominated and, frequently, frustrating. I have only to glance at my diary for 1983–84, for example, to see that a part of almost every working day was occupied either by committee meetings or by contacts with one or other of the external bodies – LEA, NAB, EARAC, HMI, CNAA, BTEC, City & Guilds – which affected the college's activities. As often as not, Geoff Wainwright exerted a much appreciated calming influence from County Hall. Internally, the college's committee structure was to some extent a product of these external forces, especially from the CNAA. If my memory serves me correctly, we had a separate Board for CNAA Courses, as well as Faculty Boards of Studies, a Board for Academic Services, a Research Committee, a Resources & Academic Policy Committee, a Staff Development Committee and a Validation & Evaluation Committee – all this for a college with no more than about 250 full-time members of teaching staff!

The 1982–83 CNAA institutional review was probably a turning-point in the college's history. It took place at a time when there was much talk about concentrating higher education in fewer institutions, notably the larger polytechnics. Colleges with only a handful of CNAA-validated programmes started to look vulnerable. I feel sure I was not alone in believing that one or two CNAA members were set on closing down degree work at Luton. On the day, matters were not helped by a dramatic start to the proceedings. This involved what I imagine must be the most disastrous cup of coffee ever served at the college. Arnold Goldman, who was chairing the visit, took a sip from his cup, paled visibly and shouted: "Stop, the coffee is poisoned!" Urgent investigations, with much toing and froing, eventually revealed that the cups had been washed in a faulty dishwasher which had failed to rinse away all the detergent. I understand that Arnold, no doubt with some embellishment, made reference to this in a short farewell speech at the end of his last institutional visit – to Harrow College in which Tony Wood participated.

Poisoning apart, my main recollection of this period is one of producing a thousand and one policy statements. Along with colleagues concerned with the DMS and the BSc (Hons) Science course, I became something of an expert on problems facing colleges with small amounts of CNAA-validated work. Frank Sutton was a tower of strength. Degree programmes at Luton survived . . . and look what happened to the CNAA.

When I come to think of it, drafting reports and writing generally has occupied a fair slice of my working life. Putteridge Bury figures prominently in this respect for me. It provided such a haven of rest when peace and quiet were needed. I recall spending virtually the whole of one summer vacation there penning my contribution to the Open University text for course E324, Management in Post-Compulsory Education. Alan Geeson was supportive as always, but word-processing was still in its infancy. Although Mike Williams, John Marshall and David Davey were striving mightily to get us to come to terms with the IT revolution, each draft of my beloved manuscript had to be produced laboriously in longhand. Putteridge Bury also brings back other memories – Governors' meetings with Frank Lester in the chair, occasional family games of tennis, the October awards ceremony, evening concerts, sharing gossip with John Moss Jones – and it was always so easy to park in those days.

I had lunch with Roy Steed on the afternoon I left Luton to come to Bolton. He spoke affectionately about his years at the college and ended up by saying: "Bob, it's all been such fun." This took me aback slightly but, on reflection, it echoes my own experiences. It also speaks volumes about Roy's approach to life, his enthusiasm for getting things done, and the pleasure which he took in achieving exactly the result which he wanted, whether on the football field, at meetings of heads of department, in arguments with the Chief Education Officer, or on the annual Fellsman Hike. Has there ever been another principal, who with deputy in tow, walked around his college at such a cracking speed?

We laughed a lot ten or more years ago – I hope the same is still true – and for this I have at least in part to thank those senior colleagues who might appropriately be described as the "old guard", namely Keith Bentley, Griff Craddock, Henry Horner, John Howard, John Shine and Albert Thomas. In many ways, however, my happiest memories are of working with the college's leading women members – Val Dempsey, Jo Douek, "Poppy" Fisher, Jo Hancock, Jessie Manley, Pam Vachon, to name but half a dozen. Where are they now?

I remain in contact with some of the people mentioned in these reminiscences, as well as with a few others whom I have not mentioned. I wish that I was in touch with more of them. They can truly claim to have helped "to put one brick upon another". ■

Memories of a Deputy Director

JIM CLARKE

I CAME TO Luton College to be interviewed for the post of Deputy Director in 1985 as a Northern lad responsible for two large engineering departments at the Bolton Institute of Higher Education. A northerner coming south brought the inevitable comparisons of separate cultures but, notwithstanding the fears, no border guards appeared to check my credentials and I soon realised that free passage would be assured both ways. I never found the southerners unfriendly and standoffish, as I had been warned, and both the pure southerners and those with northern roots were friendly and supportive in all my dealings with them.

The interview process for the Deputy's job was tough and rigorous and one fiendishly planned by the Director, now the university's Vice Chancellor. I remember particularly the slips of paper pushed into our moist hands at the end of the first day when we were told that at some point in the dinner with the Governors we would be expected to give a presentation by way of answer to the searching questions the papers contained. My wine glass remained full at the dinner – water bright was the only liquid that passed my lips that night.

However, I got the job and made up for that initial abstention through the very many cheese and wine functions that staff members put on by way of welcome to the new Deputy. A few pints of northern bitter would have gone down better, but when in Rome . . .

Attempting to span the range of activities I was subsequently involved in brings to mind very many things, but some reflections are: organising the launch of the new Computer Centre, having responsibility for the development of the Centre for Applied Technology and Innovation from its earliest days, chairing the then Validation and Evaluation Committee, preparing staff for the critical Council for National Academic Awards review, carrying out a review of the college's engineering provision, being heavily involved in the total academic restructuring of the college, and writing the college's three-year Academic Plan. A plethora of other jobs attached to my role, all of them interesting and worthwhile.

Probably the most difficult period, when tension and uncertainty reigned, related to the struggles the college had with Bedfordshire LEA over the college's bid for independent status. I reflect on meetings of many kinds where acute tension, bitterness, tested loyalties, general unpleasantness and serious heart-searching were the atmosphere surrounding set agendas. The "corridors" were rife with gossip and lobbying and one wonders how normal college business kept going under the strain.

Its final positive effect was the harnessing of senior staff behind a clearly focused cause which created a committed team determined to win. The Director at this time was under intolerable strain and both now and then my admiration for his courage and tenacity stands high.

My whole period at Luton was marked by intense ferment in terms of examination, review, forging of dreams and targets, change on all fronts, heart-searching discussion, learning and growth. One felt part of a process from which something new and good was being created.

In terms of more personal reflections, I recall the long hectic weekend drives up and down the M1/M6. I particularly savoured the Friday evening ones which always ended with a couple of pints of that beloved northern bitter, followed on the Saturday by a long run over the equally beloved Lancashire Moors. There were, however, many pleasures to look forward to in the journey North to South. One thinks of all the new relationships and friendships forged, the great challenge of the work, the opportunities for personal growth. And what can I say of croquet on a balmy summer evening at Putteridge Bury?

All in all, a total experience I would gladly repeat if my time came over again. The experience was valuable, stimulating, challenging and immensely enjoyable. Indeed, all these forced reflections give me a great feeling of warmth and belonging as I think of Luton. It is always invidious to name people in this context when I remember so many staff who gave me excellent friendship and support, but two I would name. The first is Tony Wood, the Director I worked for. He was, to me, a source of inspiration, guidance and support but also became a good friend. I admired his courage, dynamism, energy and clear vision. The second is my PA, Jessie Manley, who put up with me for some four years and was throughout this period a professional of the highest calibre – kind, understanding and patient.

I feel privileged to have had the opportunity to work at Luton College. Its new status is well deserved and I wish it well for the future. ■

The Strategy for Independence, 1987–89

TONY WOOD

A PRIL FOOLS' DAY 1987 was when it all began. Some would say the day was well chosen, and that only a fool would have begun a process (as they would see it) aimed at destroying the very fabric of higher education. I had no sympathy with such views then, and I have none now. Nor does history give them much credence, especially, perhaps, not in Luton. For that spring day in 1987 marked the beginning of a process which was to lead, in a little over six years, to Luton College of Higher Education's designation as the University of Luton. But before that, many turbulent times lay ahead.

The notable event was the publication of a long-awaited government White Paper entitled *Higher Education – A Framework for Expansion*, which proposed that the polytechnics, together with colleges of higher education having at least 55 per cent higher education provision, should be freed from local authority control and established as independent higher education corporations. A funding body – the Polytechnics and Colleges Funding Council (PCFC) – was to be established to oversee the new sector.

The proposal was greeted with near-unanimous joy by the institutions named, and seen by the polytechnics especially as the successful outcome of years of complaint on their part about alleged local authority interference in their affairs. Local government authorities did not see it in this way – to them it was another move towards dismantling the influence of county councils in favour of more centralised control.

The White Paper proposed that the new sector should be created two years later on 1 April 1989. The higher education corporations (HECs) formed would have new boards of governors composed primarily of people from business and industry. In the event, stringent controls were implemented by the government through the articles of government of the HECs to ensure minimal representation by local councillors on the boards, so that their ability to exercise any worthwhile influence was totally emasculated. The corporations would own their buildings and assets, and function in a manner akin to businesses, in a market-led education environment.

To altruists, this sounded like heresy; a complete surrender of all those things which they held dear and which, as subsequently many staff were not averse to telling me, were the reasons they had joined – and remained – in education. It seemed that the rather grubby commercial world, with its concentration on balance sheets and on following the whims of customer demand, was destined to overwhelm educational ideals. Not all, however, saw it this way. To those of us striving, with limited success, to introduce good private-sector practice into public sector organisations, this sounded promising indeed. Unfortunately, for us, there was one small problem: Luton College was not on the list since the amount of higher education work (in simple terms defined as undergraduate and postgraduate degrees, higher national certificates and diplomas, and numerous qualifications of professional institutes), had been assessed as a little under 50 per cent of the whole, several points below the qualifying threshold of 55 per cent.

During subsequent months, the higher education world buzzed with the prospect of change of a magnitude not experienced before. As more operational details emerged, it soon became clear that the government's intention was to direct support for growth into the so-called PCFC institutions; clear that is to all except those who had resolved to oppose the changes regardless. It required but a single meeting of Luton College's Academic Board to agree that we had to find a way of bringing our institution into the new sector, if we were to avoid becoming what I subsequently came to refer to as an "educational backwater".

Fortunately, the White Paper held the promise of non-qualifying colleges being able to apply for admission to the new system if they were subsequently to achieve the 55 per cent threshold for higher education. Our way forward was therefore clear: we had to adjust the higher education:further education ratio as quickly as possible. We just had time to influence the autumn 1987 enrolment. We agreed there could be no question of our cutting back on vital local further education courses, so we resolved to stabilise those numbers and direct our main energies towards a rapid expansion of our higher education activities.

We were not so naive as to imagine that our employer and controlling body, Bedfordshire County Council, would take kindly to the idea of a group of upstart employees in the south of the county seeking to influence enrolment patterns with the aim of removing their college from the council's control. The council had been "hung" for some time, with the Labour and Liberal Democrats forming an uneasy alliance, but solidly united in their opposition to government policies. Some spirited opposition could confidently be expected.

We formed an action group of senior staff to plan and execute an amended recruitment strategy, and at the next meeting of the governors, on 3 June 1987, I brought forward a report on the White Paper, together with the following resolution of the Academic Board:

> With the publication of the recent White Paper it is evident there is to be a two-tier system of public sector higher and further education, with the deciding factor being the proportion of advanced level work.
>
> From its inception, this college has enjoyed and welcomed the support of the local authority, support which we are confident would remain should we be in the second tier. However, being placed in the second tier would, in the opinion of this Board, inevitably result in a considerable reduction in our advanced work.
>
> The College Academic Board, in furthering its policy already determined over the years of increasing the volume of advanced level work in the college, supports the Director in making every effort to achieve the required proportion of higher level work to place the college in the first tier of public sector higher education.

After some debate this was adopted by the governors. Further resolutions urged the county council's education committee to support the college's attempt to achieve the requisite proportion of higher education work, and specified that membership of the new PCFC sector should be sought at the earliest opportunity.

At this time, and until eventual incorporation in 1989, the chairman of Luton College's governors was Mr Kelvin Hopkins, a full-time senior official of the National Association of Local Government Officers (NALGO). Although not a county councillor, he had been nominated by the Bedfordshire County Council as one of its majority-holding representatives. He had a strong belief in the value of higher education, and in the need for far greater opportunities for local study, especially for those who, for reason of cost or personal circumstances, were unable to travel elsewhere to undertake the courses they wished to pursue. Despite Mr Hopkins' own party's vehement opposition to the proposed legislation, he needed little convincing that PCFC membership was far more likely to bring this about than Luton College's remaining under county council control, and he remained firmly committed to gaining it throughout the subsequent campaign. The value of his support to our ultimate success cannot be overstated.

Of the other 27 members of the governing body at this time, 11 (councillors J. M. Bailey, M. D. Hand, W. M. Johnson, F. S. Lester, Miss M. C. Shephard, R. M. Sills and S. C. Stephens, plus Dr R. Bruckdorfer, Dr L. Collier, T. Toman and R. Yates) had been nominated by Bedfordshire County

A HATFUL OF TALENT

Council, one (W. A. Hill) by Hertfordshire County Council and seven by staff (S. Ackhurst, P. Hewitt, Mrs J. Parsons, Mrs. E. M. Pringle, J. Robson, B. Roe and R.C. Walker). Other constituencies represented were industry and business (A. C. Lines and P. Hoskins), trade unions (G. Slessor), universities (Professor I. D. Morton and J. G. H. Pearce), and the Church (Revd D. Banfield). The Student Union president (Miss P. Joy) and myself as college director were ex-officio governors.

At the 3 June meeting of the governing body, the last for the 1986–87 academic session, thanks were placed on record to Mr B. Hoyle, the college's long-standing chief administrative officer, who was shortly to take early retirement. He left to run a smallholding in Herefordshire, well away from the storm that would soon break.

The governors next met in November 1987, by which time two things of particular significance to subsequent events had occurred. First, as a result of concerted effort, the proportion of higher education students had risen by several percentage points, and we were fairly confident that our January enrolments to several professional courses would take us comfortably beyond the qualifying threshold for PCFC status. Secondly, after a slow start, Bedfordshire County Council had finally begun to realise what was going on in this college in the south of the county, geographically well removed from County Hall in Bedford.

The White Paper had, of course, become a regular agenda item for the governors, and after a lengthy debate in which signs of dissent from the earlier supportive decision began to surface for the first time from some of the governors, the county assistant education officer, Mr Geoffrey Wainwright, addressed the meeting. He urged caution, indicating that many features of the operation of the proposed PCFC were still unknown, and suggesting that there was plenty of time left to determine what would be best for the college and for Bedfordshire. He reported that Bedfordshire County Council had still to take an official view on the White Paper proposals. The local education authority (LEA) might, for example, decide to assist Luton College to become a non-LEA institution should this seem the best way forward. Few of us listening felt this to be a likely outcome.

Within a month a group of council governors had exercised their right to call a further meeting to discuss this issue. Still the local authority had failed to come to a policy decision on the matter, choosing instead to await "further information", and urging widespread discussions but not actually organising them. In fact, it was only some months later, after the government deadline for letters of intent from aspirant colleges had passed, that the LEA finally annnounced it was totally opposed to the introduction of the PCFC sector. Those with timid hearts would have awaited that decision and thereby lost the opportunity to apply for a change of status. There was, however, not the slightest chance we would be so foolish – our letter,

56

indicating that we intended to submit a formal application in due course, was sent to the secretary of state for education and science in good time, without reference to the local authority.

By the time we reached the next scheduled meeting of the governing body, in March 1988, things had heated up considerably. The chairman notified governors that further emergency meetings were likely in view of the mounting wave of opposition coming from Bedfordshire County Council.

The first of these, held on 20 April, was the stormiest on record, the likes of which had never been seen before and, thankfully, have never been seen since. A small number of councillor governors challenged the governing body's right to go against the wishes of the LEA controlling body. They demanded that the earlier resolution of support for the college's elevation to PCFC status be set aside, with a view to the governors not proceeding with the formal letter of application to the secretary of state. Arguments became so heated that the chairman adjourned the meeting for a short cooling-off period. When it reconvened, the earlier resolutions were confirmed, to the disgust of the opposition. Our hard preparatory work behind the scenes had paid dividends.

Within a month, the rebels had called another emergency meeting, tabling a motion aimed at overturning the earlier decisions. In heated and bitter exchanges, for which the description "ranting and raving" readily springs to mind, the arguments were rerun for the fourth time, and for the fourth time the rebels were defeated, this time by an increased margin of 19 votes to four with some abstentions. The dissident governors were incensed and demanded that their names be recorded in the minutes. This was done, and there they remain to this day.

Once again Kelvin Hopkins exercised masterly chairmanship of the proceedings. To counter accusations from the county council that the college governors were acting beyond their powers, he had written to the Department of Education and Science requesting a ruling as to whether or not this was the case. At a crucial stage of the debate he produced the official reply, which confirmed that the governors were completely within their powers. This came like a blow to the solar plexus to those who had suggested otherwise. They had been very effectively beaten at their own game. So after revisiting the original decision on three further occasions, the college formally submitted an application to join the PCFC sector.

We now entered a new phase – for me a rather nasty one. At successive subsequent meetings of the county council's education committee and further education sub-committee, some of the aggrieved members made a series of vitriolic personal attacks on me alleging unprofessionalism which, if made outside the privilege of the council chamber, could certainly have led to actions for slander.

A HATFUL OF TALENT

Particularly regrettable was a speech made by one of my own members of staff, a staff governor, who was the Bedfordshire teachers' representative on the education committee. A minority of staff members, himself included, opposed the drive to be free of the LEA. As a governor, he had had ample opportunity to advance his arguments during the many debates but, in view of my presence, had presumably lacked the courage to do so. His usual response to voting had been to abstain. He now chose instead to make swingeing statements in the chamber supposedly "on behalf of" the staff as a whole, a clear misrepresentation of the views of his constituency which he had failed to ascertain. As the subject was now rarely out of the local newspaper, his comments were widely reported. Several months later I told him I could see no real future for him in the college.

The further education sub-committee resolved that I had exceeded my authority and should be called to account. I was therefore summoned to attend a disciplinary hearing with the county council chief executive and the chief education officer. The press had a heyday, publishing headlines quoting councillors calling for me to be sacked. It was not a comfortable time.

However, I remained confident of my ability to ride the storm for two reasons. First, because I had followed meticulously the wise parting advice given to me by my predecessor, Dr Roy Steed, just before he handed over the directorship of the college to me in January 1985. Ensure you know, and follow to the letter, the articles of government, he had said, and you will avoid all major pitfalls. How right he was, for although the county council was my employer, it was to the governors that I was responsible for the academic leadership and management of the college. By keeping the governing body behind me – the second reason for my optimism – I had managed so far to perform a careful balancing act which, given a fair wind, should enable me to avoid being nailed to the mast, something my employers undoubtedly wanted to do.

Thus it was that, one day in early June 1988, I met with the two most senior officers of the county council to account for my actions in allegedly going against the clear instructions of my employers. For the first and only time in my life I called in a representative of the Association of Principals of Colleges, to which I belonged at the time. We spent some time preparing my case, thoroughly rehearsing my rationale for acting in accordance with the wishes of my governors regardless of the views of my employers. This certainly paid off, and the attempt to remove me from office subsequently sank further and further into the sand. In the way of many things, I have found, with the public sector, the matter was never really resolved one way or the other, and was in due course replaced by an alternative course. To be realistic, it was hardly likely that my employers would admit they were wrong even if this was the advice they were given.

STRATEGY FOR INDEPENDENCE

I subsequently received from the chief executive's office a most thorough and detailed record of the interview (which was quite a long one – an hour or so). This came as a considerable surprise since no-one apart from the four participants mentioned had been present, and no notes had been taken. The only possible explanation was that the conversation had been tape-recorded. No microphone or recorder had been visible, and no mention had been made of the fact that a recording was taking place. Perhaps it should not have come as such a surprise, as I was aware that the chief executive was a lawyer by profession, but it is hardly a practice that can be condoned.

Within a month of this meeting we received an official letter stating that the secretary of state for education, Kenneth Baker, had decided "provisionally" to admit Luton College to the new sector. I had the letter framed and hung in my room. The "provisional" aspect was to permit time for objections to be raised, and for ministers to review the decision in the light of any that were received.

The opposition of Bedfordshire County Council now moved into a third phase, with motions passed, letters sent, and delegations despatched – all expressing vehement objection. Feedback received through our friendly undercover network suggested that all such approaches were given a frosty reception by the then minister responsible for higher education, Robert Jackson.

We countered opposition by circulating a letter under my signature to hundreds of key businesses in the county, appealing to them to support their local college and urging them to write to the secretary of state supporting the proposed change of status. Many did, to great effect. The county chief education officer, Peter Browning, was incensed, but as I told my senior colleagues at one of our regular meetings, the gloves were off, and it was now all or nothing.

We also harnessed the support of our local members of parliament under the leadership of the MP for Luton South, Graham Bright. Our own industrial governors themselves organised a delegation of business people to the minister to argue our case. The delegation was very well received. The minister later told us how impressed he had been with his visitors and the case they had made. Apparently, he found it especially surprising and persuasive that one governor member of the delegation, George Slessor, was also a senior officer of the Amalgamated Union of Engineering Workers.

As the pace of our counter-campaign increased the chief education officer became even further incensed. I assume he was under considerable pressure from councillors to sort us out. In a stiffly worded letter, he demanded that I refrain from any further communication with anyone on anything to do with Luton College and its future, and insisted that I passed all correspondence I received to him unanswered. It was a ridiculous request and I ignored it. We carried on the hard lobbying. As the time approached for the provisional decision to be confirmed (or otherwise), I wrote a "Don's Diary" column for the *Times Higher Educational Supplement* which referred to the supposed information blackout. This attracted much interest in the higher education sector.

In late October 1988 I was in the USA as a guest of the State University of New York when I received an urgent telephone call from my deputy, Dr Jim Clarke. The chief education officer's department had just contacted him to inform the college that he was sending in the auditors the following day, and requesting full cooperation. Their mission was not financial – they had been ordered to comb through the statistical returns we had made to the Department of Education and Science concerning our student numbers which, among other things, validated our claim that Luton College had now exceeded the 55 per cent higher education qualifying criteria for PCFC membership.

What, my deputy asked, should he do? Give them full cooperation, I replied, we have nothing to hide. Nor did we. What we had done was to play absolutely by the rules, but to squeeze every ounce of benefit from them. I doubted we could be challenged. After two days, apparently somewhat dispirited and with little appetite for their thankless task, the auditors gave up and we heard no more from them. I enjoyed the rest of my stay in the USA.

In December 1988 I received a copy of a letter sent by the secretary of state to the chief executive of Bedfordshire County Council, confirming his earlier decision that Luton College would be removed from LEA control the following April. I took down the earlier letter, framed the new one, and put it on the wall where it stayed for some years. The champagne corks finally popped. It was a sweet victory.

Each academic year, in the autumn, I produced a director's report on the previous 12 months' activities for the governors. In common with practice at other LEA colleges, this was always circulated to members of the county council's education committee, following which the chairman of governors and myself were invited to attend the next meeting of the committee formally to present it.

I deliberately delayed completing my 1987–88 report until the secretary of state's confirmation had been received. In view of this decision my job now appeared reasonably secure for the immediate future, and I was able to set down rather candidly my views of the events of the previous year. In particular, I included a section which described what I felt were the obligations of that minority of governors who had sought to sabotage, by fair means or foul, the wishes of the great majority. Perhaps wisely, both my chairman and I decided to be otherwise engaged when the report was discussed by the county council's education committee. We gathered later that several councillors went nearly apoplectic when these comments were drawn to their attention. The education committee refused to accept the report, probably the first and only time this has happened in the history of the Bedfordshire LEA.

For a few brief weeks over Christmas 1988 we felt we had finally rid ourselves of the continuous programme of destructive political opposition mounted by councillors, and we could at last wholly concentrate on detailed plans for our incorporation the following April. It was particularly important we should do this. For 18 months we had waged a campaign for independence which had almost totally consumed our collective time, whereas the rest of the new sector had been busying itself with the operational details which had to be worked out after incorporation to PCFC status. It was especially galling to observe that a few other colleges that were statistically in a similar position to Luton College, had had no opposition from their LEAs. Indeed some, like Salford College of Technology (whose controlling council had a Labour majority), had benefited from local councils mounting delegations to the minister in support of their colleges' efforts to join the new sector.

In Bedfordshire, the calm was but a brief respite. With less than two months to go to vesting day, the county council launched phase four of the campaign against Luton College's plans.

The Education Reform Act required that all assets held by a college moving into the new sector at midnight on 31 March 1989 be transferred to the appropriate new higher education corporation formed at that time. Not long after the original legislation had been drawn up, it became clear that some councils might attempt to retain some of these assets by transferring ownership away from the institution before vesting day. In one celebrated case, a council fenced off a polytechnic car park to claim it as its own. To forestall such actions, the government moved quickly to give immediate protection to all those institutions listed for transfer. The problem disappeared overnight in most places – but not in Bedfordshire.

Hawk-eyed county council solicitors in Bedford had spotted a loophole: the new ruling strictly related to those polytechnics and colleges on the original list. Late entrants, like Luton College, were being admitted under a different clause in the legislation, to which this emergency legislation appeared not to apply. Without any reference to the college authorities, the council resolved to transfer immediately one of our smaller campuses, primarily used for further education activities, to a local college of further education, thereby maintaining it under LEA control.

The first we heard of this was a headline in the local paper. I took immediate action and hired some expert property solicitors to act on our behalf. We sought a High Court injunction to stall the transfer. This was granted, and subsequently a judicial review took place. The local press again had a field day, for there were few precedents for a college taking its own local authority to the High Court.

We won our case on all counts, and were awarded full costs against Bedfordshire County Council. In his summing up, which ran to 21 pages, Mr Justice Kennedy declared invalid the council's decision to transfer the property from Luton College.

He said "almost everything" about the way the decision had been taken made it impossible for him to be satisfied it had been done on valid educational grounds untainted by irrelevant considerations. He said the timing of the decision rendered it suspect. It was the second proposal within a short period to have the effect of substantially reducing the property which would otherwise have passed to the new Luton College management, a body which had accused the council of asset stripping.

The court case represented the dying gasp of a beaten adversary. That it should have come to such a pass was wholly regrettable, for before 1987 Bedfordshire had tried hard, with limited resources, to support Luton College as best it could. Relationships with council officers and councillors had been good and generally constructive. Some would say that the officers only did what the councillors told them to do. That may be technically correct, but as professionals they were in a position to advise members what would be best for the college, the county and more particularly for the people of Bedfordshire, whose councillors were there to serve them. From the moment the 1987 White Paper was published, it should have been clear to anyone with a modicum of vision what the future of higher education would be outside the new sector. Whether they lacked the vision, or chose to set it aside because of political pressures, we may never know.

In acting the way they did, the county councillors succeeded in doing two things of particular note which should serve as their legacy. First, they forced us to concentrate nearly two years of management time on fighting the campaign for our freedom. As a result of this, the amount of preparation we were able to make for the awesome new responsibilities we were to assume in April 1989 was minimal. There was little time to establish systems, appoint staff, and create the necessary structures to replace all the functions previously discharged by the council on our behalf. Over four years later, when Luton College of Higher Education became the University of Luton, we were still experiencing the adverse effects of inadequate preparation. This was their perverse legacy.

However, they left another which, paradoxically, turned out to be a potent force in shaping our future success. Against all the odds, we had overcome a succession of obstacles which many had felt were insurmountable. From the beginning, we knew exactly what we were aiming to achieve, and the time frame in which we intended to achieve it. The goal was clear, and the need to attain it for the future well-being of higher education in the area, understood. Once we had convinced the majority of our staff of this, we created an unstoppable tide of momentum. As each new barrier appeared, we had confidence we would find our way around it or over it.

Within days of our new-found independence, a reception was held at Lancaster House in London for chairmen, vice-chairmen and chief executives of the new higher education corporations. I attended with our new chairman, Professor John Matthews, who was also the Director of the prestigious agricultural research institute at Silsoe, Bedfordshire, at the time, and our vice-chairman, Tony Lines, Personnel Manager at Vauxhall Motors, and a long-standing supporter of the college. As we moved along the line of people to whom we were being introduced, we reached Robert Jackson who, as higher education minister, had been responsible for providing the final advice on our application to the secretary of state for education. He recognised me at once. In words reminiscent of the Second World War he said: "Glad we got you out of there." You can say that again, I thought.

A Polytechnic Lost:
A University Gained

TONY WOOD

NDEPENDENCE from LEA control was not the only significant event for the institution in 1989. It was also the year in which the course approvals system, administered by the Department of Education and Science (DES), was abandoned. Independence opened doors which would otherwise (for the foreseeable future) have remained closed. Without it the college could not have competed effectively for funds or students; it would have been unable to attract and retain high calibre staff, especially those having research expertise which was to prove so critical later. It would have remained an LEA further education college until 1993 when new legislation established the independence of these institutions. Thereafter, as happened with the only other college in Bedfordshire supporting significant higher education, it would then no doubt have been merged with a university centred elsewhere, and local control would have been surrendered.

Independence was a sine qua non to future success, but so was the dismantling of the DES's national course approvals process, which had so favoured the established polytechnics for more than 20 years. In essence, the system was conceived to avoid institutions duplicating courses using public sector resources when spare student places existed elsewhere. In practice it was used by the polytechnics to prevent any of the developing institutions, such as Luton College, from introducing almost any new courses at all. It was an insidious system if you were on the wrong side of it. Fortunately for the development of institutions like Luton College, it was also anathema to the Tory doctrine of market forces, and the government despatched it to the dustbin of history in 1989 as part of the higher education reforms. With that constraint gone, the college had gained a second element of freedom, and planning could begin in earnest.

One of the requirements of Polytechnics and Colleges Funding Council (PCFC) membership was that each institution had to prepare a three-year strategic plan which addressed all aspects of development and growth.

A HATFUL OF TALENT

The nub of such a plan is first to set your longer-term goal and then to work out how to move the organisation from its current position to the new one within the time frame specified. Although, in common with almost every other higher education institution, Luton College had never created a strategic plan as such in the form and detail now required, we were not unused to approaching our planning in this particular way. The most obvious recent example had been the campaign to join the PCFC sector, where the goal had been clearly established in 1987 with a two-year planning horizon.

As in 1987, it was simplicity itself to define the goal: to become a polytechnic within three years. We were quite certain our development would be permanently limited were we not able to promote ourselves under the polytechnic title. The polytechnics had been established 20 years previously and had become impressive counterparts to the universities. Their directors, however, never ceased to complain that they were disadvantaged in trying to compete on an equal footing with universities while they lacked the same title. Those of us in the colleges of higher education (HE) would have been glad to have had that particular problem for there was widespread ignorance among secondary-level teachers, parents and school leavers as to what such colleges were, and how they related to and differed from further education (FE) institutions.

Although the HE colleges battled with some success to improve their collective identity in subsequent years, culminating in 1993 with a campaign to call themselves "university colleges", the handicap of title was never resolved fairly. So the goal of polytechnic status remained pivotal.

It was, however, initially difficult to determine the steps necessary to achieve this status. Some of the very large colleges had, from time to time, sought the title but the DES had resolutely refused to create any more polytechnics since the last designation nearly 20 years earlier. Part of the problem was that nobody really knew what a polytechnic was, and without a definition it was not possible to say what had to be done to become one.

Those of us considering such matters in 1989 felt the momentum for change in higher education was unlikely to slacken for some time, and in due course some criteria must emerge. Meanwhile, common sense suggested that the best approach would be to analyse the profiles of the existing polytechnics, look for similar features, and then see how we differed.

First, polytechnics had a strong commitment to vocationally directed education, as did Luton College. However, this encompassed a much wider range of subjects than ours, as we still remained firmly rooted in the subject areas derived from the former Luton College of Technology many years previously. Other factors related to the nature of the student body. Like Luton College, most polytechnics had a strong commitment to part-time study, but they had also built up considerable numbers of full-time and sandwich students during the 1970s and 1980s. In 1989, polytechnics commonly had 4,000 to 5,000 full-time undergraduates. By comparison, Luton College had fewer than 300, all following a single degree in science.

The final characteristic was that all polytechnics (plus a small handful of the large, polytechnic-aspirant colleges) held accreditation for taught courses from the Council for National Academic Awards (CNAA). This conferred on the recipient institutions considerable powers of self-validation for new programmes of study, and was accepted as national recognition of the ability of these institutions to guarantee academic standards, without the need for close external scrutiny.

We were therefore faced in our planning with three major tasks: to widen our subject base, to increase tenfold the numbers of full-time undergraduate students across this broader range of subjects, and to obtain CNAA accreditation. Squaring up to any one of these would have been a formidable task; dealing with all three seemed to demand the impossible. Nevertheless, buoyant from winning our independence we went forward with confidence, and these three objectives formed the anchor points for our first strategic plan.

This period corresponded with the movement of my deputy, Dr Jim Clarke, to the London Institute as head of the College of Printing, and Dr Dai John, then vice-principal of the North East Surrey College of Technology, was appointed in his place. Although Dr John was unable to join the full-time staff until the start of the new academic year, with the generous support of his principal an agreement was reached whereby he began on a part-time basis for the summer term, with the specific remit of creating our first strategic plan. This he did in an exemplary fashion. Before the summer was out, the plan was written, approved by the governors, and submitted to the PCFC.

As 1989 gave way to 1990, belief that the college could indeed become a polytechnic visibly grew, and with it staff commitment to the vision. The number of sceptics rapidly declined, either through conversion or early retirement. Some had never been comfortable with the general direction in which the college was going and could not empathise with the government's market policies for education.

Midway through our 1990 plan, the DES defined the characteristics of a polytechnic, and specified the criteria for designation. These were:
- A minimum of 4,000 full time/sandwich HE students, to include at least 3,000 on undergraduate/postgraduate courses;
- 1,500 part-time HE students;
- 300 full-time HE students in each of at least five of nine designated subject groupings specified by the PCFC;
- CNAA accreditation for taught courses.

A HATFUL OF TALENT

Our earlier guesses about these requirements had been remarkably close, and the necessary adjustments to our plans were easily incorporated to keep us on target for possible designation in 1992. Little did we realise that the dealer was soon to produce a joker from the pack, put there by the polytechnics themselves.

The polytechnics had become a strong force in British higher education. Their total enrolments gradually overhauled those of the universities, and they attracted well-deserved praise from government ministers for their ability to expand and develop successfully on fairly slender resources. The time for rewarding them was approaching.

Since gaining independence, they had mounted a concerted campaign for the removal of distinctions between themselves and the universities, and for the right to call themselves universities. They claimed that there were marketing disadvantages in carrying a title which many perceived as reflecting lesser worth than the universities. This was especially so overseas. In 1991 they finally won their battle when the government decreed that all polytechnics could request a change of title to university the following year. All soon made it clear they would be doing so. Simultaneously, the CNAA would be closed down and the new universities would be empowered to award their own teaching and research degrees.

In a letter to the HE colleges, the secretary of state for education announced that no new polytechnics would be created, and that the designation would effectively die as the existing institutions were renamed. This seemed a severe blow for us, for, as a result of a phenomenal programme of course development underpinned with extensive new staff appointments and outstandingly successful recruitment campaigns over three successive intakes, we were well on target to meet the statistical requirements for polytechnic designation by the target date of September 1992. In addition, we had worked hard since 1989 to establish a comprehensive (and we felt effective) system of quality assurance which caused us to feel optimistic that we could achieve CNAA accreditation.

In the event, we became accredited as planned, and we did meet all the requirements by autumn 1992. By that time, however, the goalposts had moved. Luton had lost its polytechnic, this time by a matter of months.

However, a lifeline quickly appeared in the form of a statement by the government that HE colleges meeting certain criteria could also request a change of title to university. Proposals followed which were submitted for wide consultation.

One organisation consulted was the Standing Conference of Principals and Directors of Colleges of Higher Education (SCOP), whose membership included almost every HE college in England and Wales. As director of Luton College, I had been elected chairman of SCOP in 1990, a position I held until the college left to join the university equivalent (the Committee

The route to university status

1989
April Luton College of Higher Education incorporated as an independent higher education corporation. Academic Board introduces first phase of new quality assurance procedure.

June Governors adopt first strategic plan and agree September 1992 target for becoming a polytechnic.

September Department of Education Course approvals system ceases.
 First new undergraduate course launched for nearly 20 years.
 Significant increase in higher education student enrolments.

1990
April New quality assurance systems fully operational.

September Major range of new undergraduate and postgraduate courses introduced, accompanied by a substantial expansion of staff numbers.
 Increase in student enrolments one of the largest in the sector.

1991
September Further undergraduate/postgraduate courses launched, with enrolments again topping the sector.

December Government announces forthcoming dissolution of the binary line.

1992
May College obtains accreditation for taught courses from CNAA.

September Substantial increase in new HE programmes and enrolments again one of the highest in the sector, for the third successive year.
 College meets all the former requirements for polytechnic designation, and student number requirements for university designation.
 Privy Council grants college taught degree awarding powers.

1993
April Following a visitation by the Higher Education Quality Council, the Privy Council grants the college powers to award its own research degrees.

May Governors decide the name of the new university. Following wide consultation, no objections are raised.

June Governors apply to the Privy Council for change of title.

14 July Privy Council Order made. University of Luton established.

of Vice-Chancellors and Principals of Universities) three years later.

SCOP played a key role in helping to shape the new criteria, ensuring that any HE college wishing to work towards redesignation as a university had a fair opportunity to meet the requirements when compared to those earlier colleges – Dorset, Ealing/Thames Valley, Essex/Cambridge, Humberside – that had achieved university status through first becoming polytechnics.

The requirements for a college to seek a change of title to university were eventually agreed as:

- powers, granted by the Privy Council, to award its own taught and research degrees;
- 4,000 full-time equivalent (FTE) HE students, with 3,000 of these on undergraduate/postgraduate courses;
- 300 FTE HE students in each of at least five of the nine programme areas designated by the funding council at that time.

These requirements were substantially similar to the earlier requirements for polytechnic designation, with one important difference: the need to hold powers to award research degrees. Two-thirds of the polytechnics had never had research degree accreditation from the CNAA yet with their transition into universities they were all given their new powers automatically. For aspirant HE colleges, a new and somewhat daunting hurdle had now appeared which would ultimately have to be negotiated. Unfair it might be, but the new game could only be won by playing to the new rules.

At the time, however, we were rather preoccupied in meeting the requirement on taught degree awarding powers. We achieved CNAA accreditation for this early in 1992, and this was duly converted into the requisite powers by the Privy Council later, acting under the new arrangements. With that out of the way, we switched our attention to research degree awarding powers, resolving to make our preparations for an application early in 1993. This was successful at the first attempt.

All that then remained was to seek statements from the universities' funding council authenticating our student numbers, deciding what we wanted to call ourselves, putting our proposed name out to consultation to give the opportunity for any objections to be raised, and formally submitting a request to the Privy Council for a change of title. From that point we knew it should only be a matter of time.

While we waited, we could at last indulge ourselves by planning some celebrations. The achievement had been possible only as a result of outstanding teamwork over a number of years, and there were many people to thank including staff, students, governors, advisers, industrialists, college friends and numerous others.

The Great Putteridge Bury Garden Party was planned for Thursday 15 July 1993 in the hope that the designation of the new university would be through in time. So it was, but only just! For 24 hours earlier, on 14 July 1993 (the anniversary of the storming of the Bastille) a fax was received from the Privy Council bearing the good news. The view generally held was that this was not bad timing.

Nearly 2,000 staff, governors and their families attended a wonderful afternoon of festivities on which the sun shone. The following evening, in the marquee, a Grand Formal Ball was co-hosted by the chairman of governors, Professor John Matthews (now also the pro-chancellor of the university) and the new vice-chancellor, for governors, senior staff and many individuals and organisations outside the university who had contributed to the success. During the evening, the chairman switched on the commemorative illuminated fountain in the grounds of Putteridge Bury, simultaneously igniting a trio of giant star burst rockets – a somewhat hazardous event as it turned out.

Although Student Union representatives attended both events, the academic year for most students had finished some weeks earlier, and the students' celebrations were held early in the following term. Tributes were paid to the current Student Union President, Jon Moore, who had ensured the student body had played a major constructive role in the college's success in obtaining university status.

The Strategy for Expansion, 1989–93

DAI JOHN

WHEN IT WAS incorporated as an independent higher education corporation on 1 April 1989, Luton College of Higher Education barely satisfied the eligibility requirement for transfer from local education authority (LEA) control into the new Polytechnics and Colleges Funding Council (PCFC) sector. This was a minimum higher education (HE): further education (FE) ratio of 55:45. Indeed, the college was not originally included in the list of institutions that would transfer. There were just over 3,000 full-time equivalent (FTE) students, with part-time attendance accounting for about 65 per cent of these. The restricted range of HE programmes was dominated by Business & Technician Education Council (BTEC) higher and professional awards, and there were fewer than 300 students following first and higher degrees. This profile – and the fact that much of the Park Square campus was at that time ill-suited to HE work – contributed to a widely held view that, on paper at least, Luton College was perhaps the weakest of the "general" PCFC colleges of higher education.

The character of the FE and HE provision in 1989 was almost exclusively vocational, as the academic organisation of the college at the time made clear: there were four faculties – Applied Sciences, Business, Construction, and Engineering – and three professional centres – Accountancy Studies, Management Studies, and Applied Technology and Innovation.

Like many former technical colleges, Luton College had evolved to meet the needs of its catchment area – in this case the Luton–Dunstable–Chiltern conurbation with a population approaching 300,000 and the largest manufacturing concentration in southern England outside London. The post-war economic dynamism of the area had attracted ethnic minorities that accounted for about 20 per cent of the total population. The cultural attitudes towards gender traditions of these communities, and the type of employment to which the college's courses related, help explain a 1989 male:female ratio of about 70:30 in the student body.

A HATFUL OF TALENT

Incorporation and the first strategic plan, 1989–92

The imperatives of Luton College's first strategic plan 1989–92 (required by the PCFC of all its institutions), were survival through growth, and growth through course rationalisation and diversification, in what was already a highly competitive environment for full-time (FT) and sandwich course (SW) students, particularly in science and technology. The college believed, moreover, that the region it served was worthy of an HE institution of polytechnic status, and so this was seen as a logical extension of the growth strategy, and prioritised as a key objective.

Thus the college authorities set a target for an expansion to roughly 5,000 FTE students in 1991–92, the end of the first planning period, with almost 500 of these deriving from a formal association of the college with the Bedfordshire College of Nursing, with which it was hoped it would eventually merge. It was decided to stabilise the FE component throughout, and to sustain part-time attendance at just over 60 per cent of the gross. Effectively the objective of the plan was to double the recruitment of part-time HE students. This was in accord with the government's much-publicised views on the need to increase participation rates among non-traditional groups, through more flexible forms of delivery. It also reflected the fact that growth of FT and SW modes of attendance was in practice tightly controlled by the way core funds were distributed to public sector HE institutions. The mandatory fee per student of £607 paid by LEAs on top of these central funds was insufficient on its own to allow more than a small number of "fee-only" students to be recruited. In other words, the bulk of the planned expansion was to have been funded either by employers and/or by their employees directly, as they sought to enhance their career prospects through enrolment in part-time vocational courses.

This vital need to secure funds for growth from sources other than those controlled by central government and the Bedfordshire LEA caused the college to commit itself to a major development of contract research and, more especially, full-cost bespoke training for employers. Additional resources were to be had through competitive bids and tenders to various funding agencies, particularly those sponsored by the European Community and the then Training Agency, and so the college rapidly equipped itself with the capability to exploit these opportunities. It was decided that if the aims of the initiative in question were consistent with the college's mission and strategic direction, then every effort would be made to produce a successful application for funds. Collectively, income from these external agencies was targeted to yield 20 per cent funding independence, as a proportion of corporate revenue, from the PCFC and the Bedfordshire LEA, to whom the college was still contracted for further education courses.

Polytechnic designation criteria and changes in funding methodology
During 1990, well within the first year of the strategic plan, the government announced the first explicit criteria for polytechnic designation. Quantitatively, the requirement was for a minimum of 4,000 FT/SW HE students, of whom at least 3,000 were to be registered for degree-level work, with no fewer than 300 such students within at least five of the nine defined academic programme areas. Qualitatively, Council for National Academic Awards (CNAA) accreditation for the self-validation and award of taught degrees was also required. There was also a lesser requirement relating to part-time students which the college already satisfied.

The renewed emphasis on FT and SW students was as unexpected as it was surprising. However, the government had also indicated its intention to raise significantly the proportion of per capita funding that would henceforth be provided through the course fee as distinct from that which was channelled directly through the PCFC. Thus whereas the fee for a course in the 1989–90 academic session had been £607, this was increased to £1,675 in 1990–91 and was raised to £1,775 for Band 1 (classroom-based courses) and £2,650 for Band 2 (laboratory and workshop-based courses) in 1991–92. Furthermore, the PCFC was to introduce, with effect from 1990–91, a system of bidding for growth in core funding, whereby extra funded places would be allocated to institutions on the basis of price, ability to recruit, and quality (which was determined for the most part by Her Majesty's Inspectors).

The bidding process, coupled with the recruitment of "fee-only" students thus opened the way for much faster expansion than was hitherto envisaged in 1989. Furthermore, since the financial year at that time (1 April–31 March) preceded the academic year (1 September–31 August) by five months, it was possible to anticipate the income from successful bids well before the additional students arrived. In this way extra staff could be appointed in readiness, with the remainder of the planned increase being confirmed if and when student recruitment targets were met. The first annual revision of the college's corporate plan in June 1990 accordingly took full account of the new polytechnic designation criteria.

The response to independence, 1989-90
Simultaneous with these far-reaching changes on the national scene, in its first year of "independence" Luton had opportunistically added new degree courses in business and law together with a revised and broader combined sciences scheme. This enhanced array of courses, plus a vigorous recruitment campaign, had increased overall student numbers for 1989–90 to 4,000 FTES, rising to 4,200 if short courses were included.

Other notable achievements in this period included:
- validation of the Bedfordshire Access Consortium (one of the first in

what was subsequently to become a major national movement) in partnership with the Bedfordshire FE colleges;
• formation of a Short Course Unit with standard methods of costing and pricing, and real incentives to staff and faculties to pursue full-cost qualification courses and training for employers;
• the creation of a Centre for Educational Opportunity, funded largely through external bodies as a result of competitive bidding and other forms of entrepreneurial endeavour;
• approval from the Training Agency to introduce eight new HE courses as part of the High Technology National Training Initiative. Around £750,000 would be made available to recruit, teach and in part support 200 FT students in science, information technology, engineering and management;
• a decision in principle to add significant new components to the academic base for 1991–92 onwards, spanning health and social care, languages and humanities, and media and communications;
• the recommendation by a working party involving the local District Health Authorities, that the Bedfordshire School of Nursing and the Bedfordshire Colleges of Midwifery should merge with Luton College early in 1991;
• the submission to Bedfordshire LEA of a competitive bid to integrate the HE provision and assets of Bedford College of Higher Education with those of Luton College to create a new Bedfordshire HE institution. The latter would satisfy the numerical criteria for polytechnic designation earlier than Luton College on its own; and
• agreement with the Post Office to open the Milton Keynes Business Programme in the Post Office's Training College at Wolverton in the north of the new city. The intention was to offer part-time management and, soon after, business qualification courses. The launch was scheduled for November 1990.

Organisational changes
Perhaps of greater significance than these various early initiatives was the effort that had gone into preparing the institution long-term for the sustained growth and diversification upon which the strategic plan was first predicated, and which was now to be accelerated by radical changes nationally in HE funding mechanisms. Key among these was the creation of a flatter, simpler and highly delegated management structure, capable of operating effectively with a per capita income appreciably lower than that of any other organisation in the sector – a situation which still obtained in 1994. The new academic structure is shown in Table 1.

On-line budgets were devolved to faculties, which were free thereafter to determine resource application against perceived need and opportunities, and within the framework of previously agreed corporate objectives.

As the college expanded and diversified, the intention was not simply to maintain but also, wherever possible, to improve academic standards. While this was a worthy end in itself, it would also facilitate the essential objective of CNAA accreditation for taught courses. Success on both counts was seen as a formidable task in the attenuated timescale available, since the pool of tried HE expertise – especially at degree level – was comparatively small. In the case of the Faculty of Engineering and, to an even greater extent, in the Faculty of the Built Environment, which were still overwhelmingly FE-oriented in 1989–90, it was restricted to a mere handful of individuals.

Acknowledging the pace at which organisational and professional maturation now had to proceed, the committee structure was reduced to essentials, leaving well-defined areas of responsibility and accountability

Table 1 Faculty and School structure, 1989–90

Faculty	Schools
Applied Sciences	Geological and Environmental Sciences
	Analytical and Biological Sciences
	Computer Science
	Operational Research and Information Systems
Built Environment	Crafts
	Building Studies
Business	Marketing and Behavioural Studies
	Law
	Languages, Travel and Tourism
	Business Systems
	Accountancy and Financial Management
	Applied Social Studies
	English and Communication Skills
Engineering	Electronic and Computer Engineering
	Mechanical and Production Engineering
	Motor Vehicle, Welding and Sheet Metal Engineering
Management Centre	Human Resource Management
	Initial and Enterprise Management
	Management and Organisational Development

to course committees, examination boards, faculty academic boards and a new Academic Standards Committee. Comprehensive performance indicators were introduced, including the systematic use of student questionnaires, so that thorough and consistent annual reporting could be undertaken. The validation of new courses, and the periodic review of established ones, conformed very much to conventional practice, and was heavily reliant on external peer assessment to ensure adequate benchmarking of standards. The principle of external involvement was extended through the appointment of visiting professors and visiting fellows. The wholesale strengthening of the external calibration of standards in this way was to become a distinctive feature of the academic committee structure in subsequent years.

To manage and co-ordinate the several strands of administration integral to the operation of the quality assurance system, the college appointed in 1989 an academic secretary. The post amounted to that of a proto-academic registrar, and was to lay the foundation for a fully evolved academic registry with specialist staff relating to functions of validation, examinations, annual monitoring and evaluation, and the servicing of the senior academic committees.

Linked inextricably with the underwriting of sound academic standards were the processes of staff selection, promotion and development. The college had to be unambiguous about the achievement that was expected of those seeking new posts, promotion or other professional or salary recognition. In the event it was axiomatic that primacy should attach to course design, delivery and management on the one hand, and to research, consultancy, scholarship and professional practice on the other. Approximately 60 academic staff had left the college in the months leading up to incorporation, under the LEA's voluntary early retirement scheme. The need to fill some of these vacancies, plus additional posts arising from growth, meant that Luton was in the market for relatively large numbers of new staff. By securing clarity early on about recruitment and promotions policies, the college was able to operate to a common understanding when appointing and progressing staff who would be both supportive of the college's ambitions and instrumental in their realisation.

To sustain this culture shift, responsibility for the development of individuals – and particularly for the encouragement of research, consultancy and scholarship – was vested in line managers. The role of committees was greatly reduced, to generic policy guidance, regular commentary on the volume and calibre of activities, and advice on the organisation of the corporate staff development programme.

The senior staff, heads of schools and their support service counterparts had been placed on a salary-related annual cycle of performance review and objective setting in 1989. Later in the same year, agreement was reached on the principle of introducing a similar scheme for all other staff save that it would be directed solely to career development, without salary implications. The negotiation of targets for the forthcoming year was aided considerably by the production of a summary statement of the annual corporate objectives, derived principally from the strategic plan.

A budget was set aside for centrally arranged staff development activities, an increase of several orders of magnitude on previous allocations. Similarly, faculties were obliged to earmark 1.5 to 2 per cent of their gross income for staff development. The extent of the resources now committed represented a firm declaration of intent and signalled the central role that people management would have to play in the future.

Of the remaining strategic challenges in 1989–90, unquestionably the greatest concerned the supply and suitability of accommodation. The decision was taken to commission a comprehensive accommodation survey to examine costed options for the future development of sites and buildings. In the meantime a three-year programme of internal adaptation and refurbishment was initiated; planning commenced on a new 1,000 square metre Learning Resources Centre on the site of largely redundant engineering workshops; and a four-year lease was taken out on a modern office block and a floor of office space in a nearby building for staff rooms and various administrative functions.

Bidding for growth and university status, 1990–93
Academic expansion and diversification
Bidding for extra funded student places and the advent of the much-increased fee both took effect for the academic session 1990–91. They were to have a dramatic influence on the pace and scale of expansion across the sector for the three years they were to remain in force. In each of the three annual bidding rounds in question, the college achieved either the highest, or very close to the highest, rate of increase in funded places for polytechnics and colleges. The actual rates of increase were: 1990–91, 17.8 per cent; 1991–92, 34.4 per cent; 1992–93, 28.2 per cent.

Appreciable numbers of fee-only students were also admitted, so that the overall rate of growth was consistently the highest in the country. The general pattern of expansion over the period under review is shown in Table 2.

Funding changes alone, however, could not have delivered the growth that was subsequently achieved. An imaginative marketing drive was essential, as was a programme of new-course validation of unprecedented intensity. The detail is recorded in Appendices 2a–2c, but in summary the additional provision, quite apart from the course reviews, revisions and unsuccessful submissions included:

- 1989–90 – five new HND courses often with integral HNC courses, five

Table 2 The growth in student numbers, 1987–94

Controlling Body	Academic Session	Higher Education				Further Education (Full-time Equivalent)	Total** (Full-time Equivalent)	Approximate percentage Higher Education
		Full-time/ Sandwich	Part-time	Approx. percentage degree courses	(Full-time Equivalent)			
Local Education Authority	1987–88	840	1950	20	1720	1095	2800	60
	1988–89	890	2290	20	1965	1255	3200	60
PCFE (First Plan)	1988–90	1535*	2330	25	2645	1300	4200	70
	1990–91	2020	2540	50	3250	1355	5300	75
	1991–92	3280	2510	55	4315	1150	6000	80
PCFE (Second Plan)	1992–93	4920	2650	60	5990	1340	8000	85
HEFCE (First Plan)	1993–94	7830	2230	70	8700	760***	9500	90

Notes: *Includes about 480 nursing students **Includes PICKUP ***Total grew appreciably above this across the session

new undergraduate degrees and three postgraduate diplomas;

• 1990–91 – two new Dip HE courses, seven undergraduate courses, two postgraduate diplomas and an MSc course; and

• 1991–92 – a new cross-college modular undergraduate scheme, and various component pathways, five postgraduate diploma courses and two masters' degree courses.

The range of full-time and sandwich HE courses on offer at the start of the second planning period (1992–96) as a result of this diversification, is shown in Appendix 3.

During the period 1990–92 recruitment overall went largely to plan, with the college continuing to stress the vocational relevance of its courses. A number of structural changes also occurred which were to be instrumental in establishing the academic balance of the subsequent university.

The Bedfordshire School of Nursing, and the two Bedfordshire Colleges of Midwifery merged with Luton College in April 1991 to form the nucleus of a new Faculty of Health Care and Social Studies, with operational premises at both the Bedford and the Luton and Dunstable hospitals. As one of the first national demonstration districts to pilot the Project 2000 nursing initiative, new Diplomas in Nursing and Midwifery were introduced. Cognate disciplines in Applied Social Studies were transferred into the faculty from the business area to provide a wider spectrum of opportunity.

The first of a new generation of broad-based engineering degrees commenced, and the decision taken to establish a Faculty of Design and Technology by combining the existing faculties of Engineering and Construction. The intention was to create, in due course, a main focus on higher education courses by transferring craft-based provision into the more appropriate environment of a local college of further education.

A third new faculty – Humanities – also came into being in 1992 following the introduction, a year earlier, of highly successful undergraduate programmes, including a BA Media Studies which attracted very large numbers of applicants. The potential for further development in the media and language areas in particular was felt to be very considerable and in accord with market demand.

Science provision was strengthened by further additions to the BSc Combined Science scheme, thereby raising the number of named degree pathways from 11 to 16. The HND Applied Biology was formally embedded into the combined honours structure to provide a top-up for those students who were able, and who wished, to progress without disruption or delay. This model was to be adopted widely in subsequent years.

The potential for the development of Geology and allied subjects was also radically improved following the negotiated transfer of geological technology courses, staff, equipment, and specimen collections from South London College.

A HATFUL OF TALENT

The Faculty of Business continued to add undergraduate courses which were complementary to those already well established. The Faculty remained the primary engine of the college's expansion, with roughly 1,500 FT/SW students in 1991–92. The staff had acquitted themselves well through HMI ratings and two "outstanding" course grades from BTEC moderators, despite some very difficult circumstances arising from the reorganisation and enlargement of teaching and office accommodation.

The remaining provider unit, the Putteridge Bury Management and Conference Centre, had likewise grown remarkably between 1989 and 1992, mostly being funded through full-cost work, despite the deepening recession. Part-time student numbers almost doubled in 1990–91 and all but doubled again the following year, although this had the effect of masking the decline in part-time students elsewhere in the college. For all practical purposes, the Centre for Management Studies had become a faculty, and was so designated in 1990. The Faculty of Management was to be in the forefront of competency-based management education, and was amongst the first in the country to receive Management Charter Initiative and National Council for Vocational Qualifications accreditations. In 1990, the faculty won a National Training Award for a course provided for Vauxhall Motors, and subsequently pioneered much outreach work in Aylesbury, Havering, Dunstable and Milton Keynes.

Whilst Putteridge Bury had enjoyed considerable success in attracting full-cost work, the rest of the college had not been remiss in following the lead. This achievement, particularly from such a low base and against a difficult economic backdrop, was duly recognised by the funding council through additional financial support.

Many other benefits followed from the close relationship the college enjoyed with employers. A sponsored Centre for Surface Mount Technology training and facilities for high performance liquid chromatography were good examples, whilst companies like Vauxhall Motors, Whitbread plc and British Aerospace established the first sponsored Chairs and Fellowships.

Thus the framework for academic expansion and diversification had been put in place more or less as envisaged, and although there were adjustments still to come, the college was well on course to meet the numerical criteria for polytechnic designation.

Other events and developments
Just as the rate of growth quickened, so did the momentum on other initiatives. The college gained a string of notable successes in bidding for funds from various sources. These included:
• European Social Fund income for priority courses which averaged an annual £290,000 for the four financial years covered by the plan, and which exceeded £500,000 in one of them;

82

- £1 million for a five-year Enterprise in Higher Education project from the Department of Employment, which commenced in September 1991;
- a Department of Trade and Industry (DTI) grant for £100,000 over three years to establish an Industrial Liaison Unit;
- two DTI LINK projects, under the Molecular Sensors Programme, the first ever awarded to a college; and
- a maximum grant of £150,000 from the funding council to support the further development of research.

This latter award was particularly gratifying, for it represented an endorsement of the policies implemented to stimulate a wider base of research activity. The funds were used, in part, to lease premises for a dedicated Research Centre (named after our Chairman of Governors, John Matthews, himself a productive researcher), and to establish research studentships. Further studentships were funded by the college, and the faculties progressed the appointment of professors and readers in specified areas, against stringent criteria drawn up by the Academic Board. This surge of activity was soon to pay dividends.

Overall, increases in staffing failed to match increases in the student population, as Table 3 reveals. The combined pressure of surging growth and structural change made it imperative for career review and staff development to be given high priority. This was done, and staff began to attend a wide variety of in-house events, and to participate in external peer group activities on an unprecedented scale.

To reinforce the concept of a quality culture a project called Quality Network was introduced in 1991 – the first of its kind in higher education. It stressed the importance of honesty, trust, respect, empowerment, consultation and teamwork – as distinct from systems considerations alone – and provided a reference set of beliefs and values which the institution has attempted to live up to ever since. Closely allied to this "hearts and minds" approach was the stress laid on equal opportunities. Regular awareness-raising sessions and lunch-time seminars were arranged; interviewing for equality training was made obligatory for all staff serving on interview panels; a start was made on faculty equal opportunities audits; and a major Women into HE programme was completed. Ethnic minorities accounted for around 20 per cent of the student population at this stage.

Throughout this first phase of expansion, accommodation remained an obvious constraint. Work began in 1991 on the construction of a new 1,000 square metre Learning Resources Centre, funded entirely from the institution's own revenue. This was completed in September 1992. Some financial support had been obtained to convert the old hall and adjacent areas into modern, flexi-use, large capacity lecture theatres by the same date. To release additional space the motor vehicle and welding workshops were relocated to industrial premises. All this involved considerable

Table 3 The growth in staffing, 1988–94

Staffing categories	1988–89	1989–90	1990–91	1991–92	1992–93	1993–94
Total staff	529	499	624	711	825	1007
Teaching staff	259	279**	348	362	443	474***
FTE students	3200	4200	5300	6000	8000	9500
Student-teaching staff ratio (SSR)	12:1	13:1	15:1	16.5:1	18:1	20:1

Notes: *Staff data from 1988–89 to 1992–93 are exclusive of first-time appointments, and correspond to the close of the respective academic sessions, as do the associated data for students. The staff data for 1993–94 also exclude part-time appointments, but record the position in December 1993; the same applies to the student data. Adding back part-time staff throughout would thus reduce SSRs somewhat.
**The figure excludes about 40 nurse and midwifery tutors employed by the Regional Health Authority, whereas the students to which they relate are included in the gross FTE figure. Allowance has been made for this in deriving the SSR for 1989–90.
***This figure will rise slightly as agreed new posts are filled.

expense, and the fact that the college was still able to eliminate its inherited debt and produce a small operating surplus that year, despite having the lowest unit funding in the sector, is an indication of the efficiency levels that prevailed.

Of the several other developments, two especially are singled out for attention. After a long and arduous campaign to promote the cause of Luton College, Bedfordshire County Council in late 1990 initially voted narrowly in favour of the higher education part of Bedford College of Higher Education merging with Luton rather than with either Leicester Polytechnic, Hatfield Polytechnic, Nene College, or the University of Leicester – the other interested parties. The position was complicated, however, by an amendment requiring that a three-way link involving Hatfield Polytechnic should also be explored. In the event little headway was made with this proposition, which was finally left in abeyance when the government announced that FE colleges like Bedford would, in 1993, follow their higher education counterparts out of local authority control.

In any case, polytechnic designation via merger had never formed part of the strategic vision. So it was fitting that as the first strategic planning period drew towards its close, Luton College succeeded in obtaining CNAA accreditation for taught degrees. An application for accreditation was initially made in 1990–91 which led in turn to a panel visit. The panel was "impressed with the enthusiasm, drive and commitment displayed by the staff at all levels, their widespread engagement with quality assurance processes, and the strong sense of confidence and belief in Luton College as an academic community". Nevertheless, essentially because of the fact that so many of the college's courses had been introduced recently, as had the quality assurance system itself, it was felt to be premature to recommend approval at that time. The college reactivated its application less than a year later following another cycle of academic reporting. The visit took place in March 1992, when the panel was in no doubt that a positive recommendation was warranted.

The second strategic plan, 1992–96

Luton College was now comfortably placed to satisfy polytechnic designation criteria immediately after recruitment to the 1992–93 academic session. However the Education Reform Act, which had gone into the statute book earlier in 1992, prevented this from happening. The separate funding councils for the universities and polytechnics/colleges were to be merged into a single Higher Education Funding Council (HEFCE) which would formally end the so-called binary line. More important from Luton College's perspective, all polytechnics would automatically become universities with effect from 1992–93. No new ones would be created and the criteria for university designation were amended from those which previously applied for polytechnics. The student number requirements were eased to full-time equivalents so that part-time modes of attendance would be taken into account. However, an additional condition was inserted, namely the requirement to acquire powers to award research degrees, despite the fact that over 20 of the polytechnics had never obtained such powers from the CNAA and were to become universities nonetheless. The bidding for extra funded student places was also to be discontinued with HEFCE awarding most additional places to those institutions with the lowest operating costs and/or highest quality ratings. The upper limit for such growth was set at 10 per cent.

The second plan recognised the college was still small compared to most of the polytechnics, with several discipline areas below an acceptable critical mass. Some adjustments to the academic centres were made, giving the faculty figuration as shown in Table 4.

Full-time/sandwich student numbers grew by about 1,700 in 1992–93, partly as a result of enhanced provision, further diversification, and the introduction of a modular scheme which had considerable attractions for prospective students. A new central admissions system was introduced, and the recruitment drive had been supported by a very effective marketing campaign. Enrolments on part-time courses was however, not nearly so buoyant, as a result of the prolonged economic recession and the after-effects of the UK's sudden departure from the European Monetary System.

Without the space for expansion, this continued growth in full-time student numbers could clearly not have been contemplated. Projects completed during the summer of 1992 included the Learning Resources Centre; the conversion of the college hall into a suite of lecture theatres and rooms; conversion of the Sir John Burgoyne library to teaching and tutorial rooms; conversion of an underground car park into a student social centre (aptly named in due course The Underground); redesign of the Park Square foyer; the leasing and part-conversion of a major building on Castle Street to house the Faculty of Humanities; relocation of the motor vehicle

Table 4 Faculties/Centres at the start of the 1992–96 Plan

Faculties	Professional Centres
Applied Sciences	Educational Development
Business	(Equal Opportunities)
Design & Technology	(Curriculum Staff Development)
Health Care & Social Studies	External Affairs
Humanities	(Applied Research & Consultancy)
Management	(Enterprise in Higher Education)
	(Short Course Unit)

welding workshops to a new site, and the conversion of their former premises to a reprographics centre, college bookshop, and teaching areas; creation of improved student health facilities at Park Square; transfer of research staff and students to the Research Centre, and the conversion of vacated research laboratories at Putteridge Bury. In addition over £300,000 was spent during the same period on the further improvement of staff and student work areas. It was quite a busy summer!

Just as important was the fact that the college – because of its greater size and consequent increase in capital grant – was able to embark upon a plan of equipment acquisition and renewal that began to match many of the polytechnics. Over £1.5 million-worth of equipment was purchased in 1992–93, a sum much greater than that allocated, the difference being met through profits from full-cost work and company sponsorship. Similarly, it was decided to target the spend on library resources at or above the median for the sector, and to stay at that level for the rest of the planning period.

As before, extra staff were necessary to support the increased student numbers. Research achievement or, for younger applicants, research potential, was now given even greater prominence in making academic appointments, in view of the college's impending bid for the power to award research degrees. The research output of the existing staff continued to grow with a year-on-year increase in volume and calibre that would eventually well exceed the target for the year. More research students were recruited into all faculties.

Staff development advanced on a much wider front, and work also commenced on a systematic staff database designed to provide an audit of existing expertise and, through annual updates, a record of year-on-year progress. A corporate equal opportunities policy statement and guidelines document was produced, and a database assembled to facilitate contact with professional groups of ethnic minorities, women and disabled persons, for use when advertising new posts and vacancies. With these development tools the college was at last able to work towards a balance in gender, ethnicity and disability which reflected that of the population at large. The college was also well placed to apply to the Bedfordshire Training and Enterprise Council for Investor in People accreditation, and a formal declaration of intent was made early in 1993. The successful application was made a year later when the new University of Luton became the first university to gain this recognition.

Research degree awarding powers and university status
The policies, infrastructure and procedures required to underpin a successful bid for research degree awarding powers were already largely in place well before it became apparent that Luton would need to acquire such powers as a precondition of university status. This had been done partly as

Table 5 Faculty/Schools and Professional Centres, 1993–94

Faculty	Schools
Applied Sciences	Analytical and Biological Sciences Geological and Environmental Sciences Geography and Mapping Computing and Information Systems Mathematics, Statistics and Operational Research
Business	Accountancy and Financial Management Marketing Business Systems Law Travel, Tourism and Leisure Economics
Design and Technology	Built Environment Electronics and Computer Engineering Further Education Technology Mechanical and Production Engineering
Health Care and Social Studies	Acute Health Care and Midwifery Politics and Public Policy Psychology Social Studies Community and Mental Health Care
Humanities	Language and Linguistics Literature and Linguistics Media Arts
Management	Human Resource Management Operational Management Strategic and General Management

Professional Centre	Units/Sections
External Affairs	Enterprise Commercial Affairs Unit Research Unit Cultural Affairs Unit
Educational Development	Community Projects Equal Opportunities Staff and Curriculum Development Study Support

an extension of the quality assurance mechanisms so effectively established for taught degrees, and partly as an integral feature of the long-term development plan devised for research. The additional hurdle set up for university designation, therefore, merely expedited the plan's execution.

A considered application had to await the setting up of a new national body, the Higher Education Quality Council (HEQC), which was to advise the government on future applications for degree awarding powers of both kinds following the demise of the CNAA. Criteria were eventually drawn up against which applications would be judged, and the college decided to work towards making a submission early in 1993. In the meantime, an interim arrangement was needed to validate research degrees at Luton,and the University of Sheffield agreed to undertake this task as part of a wider collaborative relationship.

The submission went forward in February, and the HEQC visited in April. The outcome was wholly satisfactory, with a clear recommendation that the institution should be given research degree awarding powers, the first to achieve this distinction under the new national arrangements. A month later, the Privy Council confirmed the powers, so that all the requirements for university designation had now been achieved. The staff had worked unstintingly to make a reality of what must have seemed to many outside observers in 1989 to be a remote, if not altogether an illusory prospect. The formation of the University of Luton represented the culmination of a remarkable phase in the evolution of higher education in Luton. It was a just and fitting reward for everyone.

The Board of Governors, 1989–93

JOHN MATTHEWS

THE IMPENDING achievement of independent status by Luton College as a higher education (HE) institution from 1 April 1989 called for the establishment of a new Board of Governors. Its members had to have time to become familiar with the background and to set up proper working procedures by that date. So in the autumn of 1988 the college Director, Tony Wood, began a wide-ranging search and extensive series of discussions to identify candidate governors. The shape and size of the Board were set by the 1988 Education Act, but this gave considerable freedom to determine its total size, while requiring that "independent" governors must be in an overall majority. Staff and students were to be represented and provision was made for local government representatives, but the latter were to be very much in the minority compared with their earlier dominance of college governance.

The first Board

Although the total Board complement could have varied from 12 to 15, provided independent governors were in an overall majority, Dr Wood considered that the vital importance for the future of the college of involving local industry and commerce as well as other professions could best be served by a wide range of governors from those sources. He thus set out to identify and recruit 13 independent governors. Many of those approached were, of course, already well known to the college as distinguished Luton and Bedfordshire businessmen and women. Prominent among those who advised and helped the Director in this search for an imaginative Board of wide experience were Tony Lines (who subsequently became Vice-Chairman), Peter Henman, Philip Hoskins, Bryan Roe and County Councillor Eric Stephens.

Independent governors, governors from local government and governors appointed from inside the college recruited by Tony Wood and co-opted members voted for at the 1 February 1989 Board meeting are listed on pages 93 and 94. Of the original 13 independent governors, nine continue to serve in 1994, a tribute not only to the original selection but also to the interesting challenge which Luton College brought to many governors' lives. Although the make-up of the First Board was predominantly male and certainly all white, the business and professional expertise was wide. Few members knew one another but comfortable and constructive relationships developed quickly, most markedly within the committees.

The Board Designate first met in late 1988 with the initial priorities being to agree a constitution and an appropriate committee structure. These more formal tasks were complemented by the challenge to set the habits – later to be regarded as "traditions" – of a constructive way of working.

Committees of the Board
The Finance and General Purposes Committee
The Finance and General Purposes Committee (F&GP) was always envisaged to have a substantial task: the magnitude of its subsequent workload was certainly not foreseen. Now it is usual for the F&GP to meet for up to four hours every few weeks – often continuing until after 10pm. At a later stage it was decided that a sub-committee to deal with property matters was needed. Both the F&GP and its Property Sub-Committee have from the first been under the skilled and punctilious chairmanship of Peter Henman. The evening meetings have often incorporated inspections of ongoing or completed building works. To regular attenders – Eric Stephens, David Palmer, Len Collier (the Luton Borough Council-nominated Governor from 1991 to 1993) and John Matthews – those meetings will be remembered for their inevitable sandwiches but more happily for the "acceptable" bottle of wine. In this context "acceptability" refers to Tony Wood's judgement that there would be no complaint from Eric Stephens, who as an ex-hotelier and continuing bon-viveur was well cast as the standards-setter. It must be added that more recently wholemeal bread and open sandwiches have been introduced to avoid "sandwich fatigue".

One severe problem for a committee with such a large workload of complex and – because of the financial dominance – vital business has been how to communicate effectively its decisions and recommendations to the full Board. With contracts, loans and, occasionally, overdrafts running to seven figure numbers and an annual budget of £40 million plus, all governors naturally feel the need to understand and judge all budgetary decisions. Yet the F&GP will often need two to three hours of study and discussion before it can reach a decision. Papers and verbal presentations for the Board have been continually refined, but the problem remains to be completely solved.

Before passing on, it is very important to understand the part played by

The Original Independent Governors

Julie Bonner Personnel Manager of Monarch Airlines, based at Luton Airport. She has continued to serve on the Board in 1994 and has brought a great deal of expertise to the Human Resources Committee as well as the Board.

David Brown Chairman and Chief Executive of the truck company AWD, which had taken over both the factory and some of the business when Bedford Trucks pulled out of Dunstable. Unfortunately, he found the pressure of business limited his college activities and he was unable to continue. Subsequently his company became a victim of the recession.

Cliff Bygrave A partner in the accounting firm of Arthur Young, he was obliged to resign his membership of the Board most reluctantly when his company through amalgamation became the official auditors of the college as Ernst & Young.

Peter Henman Chairman and Chief Executive of Luton-based building group T & E Neville. He is one of the most active governors and has been from the first the Chairman of the Finance and General Purposes Committee. Furthermore, his expertise has provided guidance to Finance and Estates staff between meetings.

Philip Hoskins Chief Executive of the Bedfordshire Chamber of Commerce, with which the college and university have always maintained a very close relationship. His membership of the Board continued in 1994.

Tony Lines Personnel Manager of Vauxhall Motors, Luton. He became Vice-Chairman of the Board and Chairman of its Human Resources Committee. Both in committee and privately he has continued to prove a constructive questioner of policies and an imaginative proposer of options.

Derek Ludlow Chairman and Managing Director of Ludlows of Luton, which has a range of business activities from automobile engineering to wine importation. He is one of many who have served the college at periods through its life to whom the title "Mr Luton" has been attached. A determined questioner, he serves (at least in the Finance and General Purposes Committee) as the archetype of the Board member who will locate any looseness in policy or its presentation.

John Matthews In 1989 he was Director of the Agricultural and Food Research Council's Institute of Engineering Research at Silsoe College. A physicist and engineer, he was elected Chairman of the Board, a role in which he had wide experience on both national and international bodies.

David Palmer A Chartered Accountant, experienced and active in training, he has contributed his professional knowledge to the Finance and General Purposes Committee.

George Slessor Deputy Head of the Amalgamated Engineering Union's branch office in Luton, he has served the college well on the Human Resources Committee and as one of the most regular governor attendees of functions. Although now retired, he continues his deep commitment to the university.

Julia Thorne A public relations expert and Managing Director of London-based Paragon Communications plc. She resigned when her professional duties increased.

Gerald Watson Managing Director of Luton company Measurement Technology Ltd. He contributed a great deal directly to the faculties as well as to the Board before resigning in 1992 on his retirement from MTL and moving from the area. He worked particularly hard to assist the Engineering Faculty.

Tony Whitear Director of Research, Whitbread plc, is head of the company's research laboratories on a site adjacent to the Park Square Campus. He is another constructive thinker and questioner who continues to serve on the Audit Committee and the Honours Panel of the Board.

Original Local Government and College Governors

Bill McKenzie A Bedfordshire County Councillor, he is also an accountant and was initially voted Chairman of the Audit Committee. However, his professional and political activities, culminating in his parliamentary candidature, led to his resignation in 1991.

Eric Stephens A Bedfordshire County Councillor, he developed a strong affinity for the Luton College before it attained independent status and, as a Governor, has continued both his perceptive questioning and his strong support since. A valued Finance and General Purposes Committee member, he has now been appointed as an Independent Governor following his retirement from the Council in 1993.

Viv Dunington A Luton Borough Councillor, he had previously served on the College Governing Body for several years and thus provided a very valuable background of experience. Another person to whom the label "Mr Luton" has sometimes been attached.

Tony Wood Director and Chief Executive, Luton College, who from the first has presented and defended his proposals with great skill and force, but has never sought to bully or belittle others.

Steve Akhurst The first representative of the teaching staff. He balanced well the undoubted concerns of many staff at the massive changes being made and the vision needed to achieve the necessary changes in culture.

John Smith Elected representative of the teaching staff of the college, he served until 1993 with great adherence to his principles and with a good contribution to the Student Affairs Committee.

Jo Parsons Elected representative of the non-teaching staff. Although not now on the Board, she continues to represent staff interests strongly as a Union Officer. **Donna Bakewell** and **Joan Drage** have followed her on the Board.

Steve Duff President, Student Union for the year 1988–89 and the first of a series of Presidents to join the Board. **Zoe Toulman, Greg Keech**, **Jon Moore** and **Chris Harris** succeeded him. These presidents have latterly become also key members of the Student Affairs Committee.

Paula Grayson Not a governor, but Clerk to the Board and Personnel Executive of the college, she has provided efficient administrative support for the Board.

Co-opted Members elected at 1 February 1989 Board Meeting

Rt Revd David Farmbrough, Bishop of Bedford He served until his retirement in 1993, bringing to the Board a strong interest in the student population and its broader experiences at Luton. His contributions to the Student Affairs Committee and the Awards Panel have been extremely constructive and effective.

Brian Houseman Principal of the Luton Sixth Form College. He has been an enthusiastic proponent of college links through the South Bedfordshire College Federation.

the Property Sub-Committee in setting up and monitoring the very large building programme, and to recognise the outstanding part played by Peter Henman. As the head of a major building company, he has been able to inject standards and targets of practicability of progress and of cost. In particular, his contracting skills and experience have probably saved the college several hundreds of thousands of pounds, while the vast majority of contracts were completed without undue mishap or delay. A worry of the Board has been that his position has so often excluded his own company from tendering for work.

The Human Resources Committee

The Human Resources Committee (HRC) has also benefited greatly from the professional skills and experience of its Chairman, Tony Lines. With two personnel managers, a senior trades union official and, usually one or two employers, as well as the Director and Personnel Executive of the college present, this group has been particularly well equipped to guide and aid the executive in the major task of changing not only the staff organisational and rewards structures, but to a large degree its culture. One great sense of satisfaction to governors is that "a fly on the wall" would not recognise the individual members' affiliations from their policy contributions. Certainly the "two-sides of industry" have never been evident, unless it be in their taking roles opposite to expectations!

Although the full Board has been more willing to accept recommendations from the HRC without detailed analysis, the committee has faced other challenges. Chief among these has been the difficulty in quantifying performance, corporate efficiency or developments. Statistics of staff numbers by grades, function, qualification, rewards or absence can be collected and examined. Time trends can be discerned and the possible reasons for trends suggested. Norms are, however, very difficult to establish on a local or national basis. Benchmarking, using other institutions within or outside the HE sector for comparison, still needs to be developed further. Although the committee and the Board are confident that the establishment and the staff are performing well, improvements attainable in many factors cannot be quantified confidently.

The Audit Committee

The Audit Committee has taken longer than others to become an effective group. It was probably only in 1992, under the chairmanship of Simon Cuthbertson, a partner at Coopers & Lybrand in Milton Keynes, who joined the Board in 1991, that its monitoring and auditing activities became sufficiently severe and constructive. The Audit Committee can now be relied upon to insist on a comprehensive response, backed by actual changes, to any inadequacy uncovered by professional audit.

A HATFUL OF TALENT

The Academic Board

There are no external governors sitting on the Academic Board, but under the Director's chairmanship it has very effectively plotted and maintained the course of academic developments of the college and nascent university. It has reported fully to Board meetings but such has been the confidence in the Director and the Academic Board with the evidence of spectacular increases in course portfolio, in quality assurance and in research, that most interjections by governors have been to seek clarification, rather than to question motive or action. Nevertheless the Board of Governors has been deeply concerned to probe forcefully the very occasional critical HMI Report, the more so perhaps because of their very infrequent occurrence.

The Honours Panel

The panel responsible for awards and honours has met annually under the Chairman of the Board to consider candidates – put forward by staff and governors – for Fellowship of the College, and also to provide the Director with advice on guests of honour for award ceremonies. The scope for awards and the work of the panel will increase with university status. Members feel satisfied at this point that, among the names suggested, they have been able to identify each year two Fellows of distinction who have been both thoroughly deserving and felt very honoured to receive the award. All have had connections with the college but the intention has been to award one Fellowship for exceptional local achievements and one for his or her national distinction. It is extremely satisfying that the first Chancellor of the University of Luton, Sir David Plastow, should, in competition with many who were considered, have been drawn from among our Honorary Fellows.

Ad Hoc panels

Ad hoc panels have been set up by governors to assist with particular challenges. Engineering courses and policies for overseas marketing are examples of the subjects tackled. Governors with specialised knowledge have been very keen to help staff and, to some extent, these short-term studies might be seen as a precursor to the later agreement for the majority of independent governors to "adopt" a Faculty or department in order to provide advice directly.

The Student Affairs Committee

The most recently formed governor's committee is the Student Affairs Committee, which was formed in 1992 with Wendy Francis, a training executive from Milton Keynes who joined the Board in 1991, as its first

Chairman. With the Bishop of Bedford, County Councillor Jim Thakoordin (Governor from 1991 to 1993), John Matthews and the staff and student governors joining, the committee has been well equipped to address problems of student welfare, social and sports activity, provisions for disabled students and disciplinary procedures, for example. It has also acted as the Board's monitoring group for Student Union activities, including the annual budget bid and has managed at the same time to provide a source of guidance and advice. This body has responded well and actively sought views from the committee, a gratifying aspect for its members.

Board meetings

With a fully formed committee structure and a large Board membership there has always been a severe risk that full Board meetings would become little more than reporting sessions. Governors have preferred to meet early in the day, normally starting meetings at 8.30am after consuming (normally very rapidly) a light breakfast, attractively provided by the Putteridge Bury catering service. Many members have needed however to depart by 11am and this has determined the length of the agenda and the depth of discussion.

A typical agenda would run something as follows:
• Membership matters and apologies are likely to occupy no more than five minutes, including a one to two minute late start;
• minutes of the previous meeting and matters arising can obviously contain substantial items, largely in the latter part, but 10 minutes is all the time that can really be allocated.
• Reports from seven committees, from the Academic Board to Putteridge Bury Advisory Committee, might encompass as many as 15–16 separate meetings to be covered. Although a later innovation has been to summarise on one sheet for each committee the principal issues for presentation and discussion, for ratification or decision and for future committee business, clearly this part of the meeting must be allocated at least one hour.
• The main items for Board debate and decision follow. With three Board meetings a year, these policy items might amount to five or six topics at each meeting. Some will occur annually, such as the Strategic Plan, Budget Approvals or Annual Accounts. Others will be major strategic items of the time; for example the policy on Further Education in the institution or, indeed, the decisions related to university status. This section of the meeting is also extremely difficult to navigate in less than one hour.
• In the first two or three years a topic was featured at each meeting in the form of a mini-seminar to provide information to governors primarily, but with some guidance through feedback. Such topics would be presented

by senior members of staff normally with visual aids. Quality assurance systems, research policy and programme, and strategic plan development were examples. With a 10-minute presentation followed by a discussion, a period of less than half an hour was not effective. With the overall meeting time constraint it has subsequently been found more practicable to deal with these topics in self-contained governors' seminars.

● The meeting agenda will then conclude with one or two items for information only and with Chairman's Announcements (comments on principal events since the last Board meeting, or scheduled before the next, award ceremonies, VIP visits, governors and college gatherings will be included, as well as honours or distinctions achieved by the institution or individual members of staff or the students).

All this explains why in 1993 four Board meetings per year have been planned for the future. It explains why Governors' Seminars have been held as a regular, if occasional, event. These have been of somewhat variable success. The staff members presenting the topics, which have varied from Equal Opportunities or Health and Safety to Further Education Policy or Strategic Planning, have prepared and performed superbly. The variable, it must be admitted, has been governor attendance, with some attracting 80 per cent of the Board and others only 20 per cent. By definition governors chosen are obviously very busy people with other professional and extramural activities. Judging and maintaining what is an acceptable commitment, with Board and committee meetings, adopted Faculty contact, formal and ceremonial occasions, plus these seminars, is one of the more difficult challenges to assess.

It is appropriate to refer again to the staff and student governors. They too carry a substantial additional responsibility and time burden through their membership. The staff members have regularly attended seminars and celebratory and social events as well as Board meetings and they serve on the Student Affairs Committee. The student representative – successive Presidents of the Student Union – has also shown maximum interest and participation in Board activities and has consequently found generally a very sympathetic forum. One must not forget the interest and, when appropriate, the participation of other members of the senior staff. They have regularly attended Board meetings as observers in large numbers and have willingly and easily fitted into other events, from seminars to formal dinners. Dai John as Deputy Director speaking on planning and policy matters, Keith Cook as Assistant Director dealing with estate and student matters, Dick Jeyes and Paula Grayson speaking on finance and personnel matters respectively and Roger Williams, the institution's legal guru and natural "Master of Ceremonies", are all known to the Board. The two Welshmen, in particular, have demonstrated the standard of eloquence for which the Principality is justly famed.

Case study – proposed merger with Bedford College

Although many important and interesting topics and decisions have come to the Board, one which still stands out as an important challenge was the attempted amalgamation with Bedford College of Higher Education. Perhaps the memory is still vivid because it was an initiative in which we failed; a rare, if not unique, example. Yet it was a failure in which we lost no real status. It can probably now be argued that, in failing and thus missing a possible change of gaining polytechnic status while that was still an option, our subsequent achievement of the more stringent targets set for direct transfer to university status, have forced us to advance more substantially and more rapidly in academic terms. The story is worth recalling as an example of the Executive and the Board performing at their best and in an excellent partnership.

Bedford College, with something over a thousand HE students, was seen to have limited viability as an independent HE institution. In 1991, Bedfordshire County Council, which was then responsible for the college, announced that it was seeking amalgamations. Luton College, with ambitious plans, naturally bid, although it was not initially short-listed – apparently our bidding papers went astray! On appeal we found ourselves in short-list competition with the then Leicester and Hatfield Polytechnics, Leicester University and Nene College, Northampton.

The Board held an Extraordinary (evening) meeting, at which senior staff were also invited to participate in order to sharpen and detail our bidding plans, and this may be recalled as one of the most constructive and helpful meetings of governors to date. The bid was essentially that there should be a Bedfordshire College of Higher Education which could soon qualify, through its student numbers and its degree course quality as a polytechnic. There would be equal status campuses in Luton and Bedford with these developing to be generally of the same scale. Not surprisingly, as both colleges had been under Bedfordshire County Council administration until 1989, the academic skills and courses were to a large extent complementary. The scheme appeared to us then, and still does, to provide Bedfordshire with a county polytechnic and later a university which would help to reduce the chasm which is often thought to exist between the two principal towns and their surrounding areas – Bedford, the administrative capital, and Luton, the industrial capital.

The Education Committee of the County Council was asked to advise the Council and requested presentations from the five organisations bidding. These were made with varying degrees of substance and "gloss". In addition, individual governors and staff used their contacts and opportunities to promote strongly the Luton–Bedford case. Yet from the first we all felt it was an uphill struggle, the reasons appearing to be:

- The lack of belief that we could achieve our ambitious plans to be a polytechnic in two years (these plans have, of course, effectively been achieved and surpassed through university status).
- The history of struggle with the County Council in 1988 and 1989 for Luton College to become an independent institution. (Even in 1990 our rapid expansion often seemed to cause more suspicion than joy in the County Council.)
- The long-standing animosity between the Bedford and Luton areas of the county (similar perhaps to the Edinburgh–Glasgow, Rome–Milan and Madrid–Barcelona relationships. The great pity was that the merger of colleges could have been taken as an opportunity to help unify the county).

It emerged that of the three political party leaders on the full council and the three party leaders on education, we had only one supporter, County Councillor Mrs Angela Roberts from Dunstable. Eventually, after intense lobbying, the college's campaign could not achieve the decision we wanted, but we did manage to achieve a situation where Leicester, the earlier front runner was put aside in favour of a period of negotiation between Luton, Hatfield and Bedford to see if an appropriate three-way partnership could be agreed (leading to a Polytechnic of Hertfordshire and Bedfordshire). The Board at Luton was happy to enter such discussions on the basis that any agreement must result in power-sharing between the two counties in such a way, that maintenance and improvement of resources and education provision could be assured for Bedfordshire in general and Luton in particular. Clearly the maintenance of a strong campus with broad subject provision in Luton would have to be a high priority of governors with a prime responsibility to the local population, industry and professions. Despite several rounds of discussion at governor/councillor and, later, executive levels, Hatfield was unwilling to share any power at Board or executive levels and negotiations lapsed. The 1992 Further Education Act gave Bedford College its independence from the County Council and in 1993, after further debate within its governing body, the decision was taken to become part of De Montfort University (the successor to Leicester Polytechnic).

In retrospect, had the Luton bid been accepted, the "University of Bedfordshire" would probably have come into being a year earlier than the University of Luton achieved its Royal Charter. It would have been through the automatic renaming of the "Polytechnic of Bedfordshire". Yet what has happened has, to the benefit of South Bedfordshire, certainly resulted in a wider range of subjects being taught in Luton and has led to the most impressive growth in expertise and systems for the teaching of postgraduate research students. Furthermore this enhancement of research activity will probably lead to a rapid gain in the quality categorisation of actual research carried out.

Review of Board activities and performance

Not all Board activity has, of course, been as exciting or as externally visible as the attempted merger with Bedford College. Nevertheless progress to university (earlier we saw it as polytechnic) status has always been rapid and on a wide front, encompassing academic courses, research and consultancy growth, staff and organisational structure development, dramatic growth in accommodation, and consequent financial challenges of the highest order. For a governor, with all these simultaneous happenings – clearly forced and controlled by a skilled and inspired executive – life on the Board and its committees could be a little like riding a giant Pacific wave. It was clear that governors all wished to give more, and at the same time could see the problems of committing their time and sharing responsibility, as well as the need to concentrate primarily on strategy. With the mixture of satisfaction with the overall progress of the college, which by then was being recognised nationally as a high flying organisation, and some dissatisfaction that not all governors were being provided with an optimum degree of interest and challenge, it was with much pleasure and enthusiasm that the Chairman and the Director received an invitation from the Committee of Polytechnic Directors to attend a residential seminar on the role of governing bodies.

This event showed that most of our concerns were shared by institutions in the polytechnic sector. Organisations with small Boards of eight to ten members and those with large Boards, like ours, compared experiences. No consensus arose on the better arrangement. Other principal issues to surface included the relationship between Chairman and Chief Executive, the avoidance of two "classes" of governors (those most involved through committee or office positions and those less involved), the appropriate period of tenure of governors, and their familiarisation and training. The result nationally at this and parallel seminars was a report to the minister on future regulations for governing bodies. Locally the seminar was important as it provided some opportunity to benchmark our own activities, and some further encouragement to explore the need for, and practicability of changes to, our own Board procedures.

It was largely as a result of this experience that the Chairman arranged for Dr Pat Ellis and her colleagues to survey the satisfaction of governors with current arrangements. This survey also set out to determine preferences on such issues as Board and committee structures, agenda and paper formats, times and frequencies of meetings, degree of governor involvement in the college and, perhaps most importantly, the apparent and actual relative decision-making responsibilities of governors and directorate. This latter point related mainly to the degree to which, in important issues, the papers and presentations by the Executive strongly led the Board in contrast to a listing of options with minimum leadership. To achieve an optimum consistency here is difficult. Probably, the more skilled the management, the more they are likely to lead the Board. As long as they are correct this is a positive factor, but the fear exists in all governors of failing to recognise an erroneous Executive policy. Fortunately, this has not occurred, but it was comforting to find in governors' responses that they place a very high priority on constructive monitoring of staff-developed strategies.

The changes made following this survey have largely been in improving training and familiarisation for new governors. As well as more opportunities for tours of the college and to meet staff and students, the Chairman meets individually with all new governors after three to six months in office. This allows questions to be raised to fill in any background to issues, policies and personalities which concern the governor and, perhaps more importantly, encourages the latter to forward reactions, opinions and impressions from the relatively fresh perspective of the newcomer to the Board.

Other developments from the survey have been the adoption by individual governors of their preferred faculty or department with direct and frequent contact, the initiation of an additional news-sheet specifically for governors, and summary proformas to introduce committees' minutes to the Board which assist in prioritising the information contained.

The growing roles of governors
An initially informal, yet now almost "traditional" small group within the Board is the Chairman's "Three Wise Men" (no sexual discrimination intended). These – Chairman John Matthews, Vice-Chairman Tony Lines and Chairman of F&GP Committee Peter Henman – have gathered two or three times annually to determine the Director's salary and performance-related pay and to advise the Director on remuneration ranges of other senior staff. In more recent years the group has negotiated with the Director on the Corporate Objectives to be set for the year, the achievement of which will be used to determine a component of all senior staff performance-related pay. At the end of the year the group has needed to quantify success, a challenge which has led to successive improvements in the quantification methodology and hopefully in the accuracy of judgements.

In addition to attendance at decision-making meetings and information-providing seminars, governors have several other opportunities to be involved in college life. The more obvious ones involve events such as student award ceremonies, launching new activities or new premises, VIP visits, and local and national events where governors represent the college. Governors met many extremely interesting people through ceremonial and VIP visit events. Parents of students, travelling from as far as South-East Asia to awards ceremonies, have favourably compared our ceremonies held in the hallowed and appropriate surroundings of St Mary's Parish Church, with those of the most distinguished universities. From listening to a jazz band in the company of the Mayor of Luton at the opening of new student union premises, to listening to the remarkably thoughtful and powerful words of Archbishop Runcie to assembled businessmen, the memories are still vivid.

An important part of the governors' role is their regular involvement in recruitment interviews for senior staff, and participation with staff in specific developments such as research appraisal or the promotion of the institution's interests through external contacts with organisations or individuals. Recruitment interviews have given many governors added and valuable insight into the ethos and the academic topics of the college, making them doubly valuable. Governor-members of interview panels have been very positive with their questions and their conclusions. Assessments have been very comprehensive and in one case a successful candidate, now a senior staff member, was told of this success but at the same time advised that his fluorescent green socks were perhaps inappropriate for such an interview!

As part of the research training quality assurance system, a Quality Audit Panel reporting directly to the Board has been established. This panel is made up of six academics from other universities who together span the subject range of the college's activity. Meetings are held twice a year to examine research training procedures and activities, to ensure that they meet standards recognised as normal within the HE sector. The Board eagerly anticipates the reports it will receive when the panel has gained a broad perspective. Meanwhile the interim views given to the Board Chairman have been very positive.

The Board's rewards

While most Board and individual governors' activities are interesting in themselves, governors' contributions have been well recognised by the college, both routinely and particularly at the time of celebrating university status. Annual "Governors' Dinners" have been held as an excellent way of showing gratitude to governors and their long-suffering partners and these have also provided a means of saying thank you to several other close friends of the college. Tony Wood has quite rightly recognised the occasion as one when appropriate guests and, particularly, guests of honour, can learn something of the college's achievements and aspirations, but can also impart to governors and senior staff words of informed wisdom which will be relevant to our councils in the year to come. Guests of Honour have included: Malcolm Frazer, Chief Executive of the Council for National Academic Awards (CNAA); Graeme Davies, Chief Executive, Higher Education Funding Council; Lord Parkinson, ex-minister and senior politician and Dr (now Sir William) Stubbs.

A HATFUL OF TALENT

These dinners have been splendid occasions at which our guests appear to have been very much impressed, not only by the surroundings and splendid ambience of Putteridge Bury, but also by the high-quality food. Among governors, the "Kitchens" at Putteridge Bury enjoy a tremendously high reputation for the originality and quality of the food as well as for the superb service.

Again the College excelled in organising the splendid celebratory dinner & dance to mark university status. This was the first of our events to be held in a marquee in the grounds, permitting a large number of guests to be invited in gratitude for the support given by themselves and their organisations. The whole evening was said by those present to be most relaxing and enjoyable, again a tribute to the special atmosphere of Putteridge Bury. This was evident from the reception, held under a canvas awning over the terrace to the celebratory launch of the floodlit fountain towards the end of the evening, which was accompanied by the firing of rockets. Putteridge Bury is near to the flight paths of Luton Airport, but fortunately the rockets did not require take-off permission from the control tower, as was the case at the celebratory garden party on the previous day when control tower permission was needed at the release of the gas-filled balloons in the balloon race. Our release "window" was a surprisingly narrow one.

A part of the dinner & dance which attracted support from all governors was the surprise presentation of gifts from governors to the Director and Deputy Director. It was perhaps the very first time that the Board did something of which Tony Wood and Dai John were not aware! It was some small reward for their extremely hard work in gaining university status.

The surprise was, on a less serious note, particularly pleasing to the Chairman and Vice-Chairman who, at an earlier staff Christmas Dinner were given presents of after-shave lotion sold as Old Welsh Sheep Dip and Sump Oil in recognition of their respective associations. Later careful comparisons of the "bouquet" suggested that both bottles contained the same fragrance.

Some reflections

This has been a very personal account of the Board of Governors at work and at play. All members have other commitments and the large majority a full-time position of responsibility. The general reaction is, however, that the Luton College experience added much interest and not-a-little excitement to already colourful lives. One can be confident that no-one holds any regrets.

After almost five years of activity, general conclusions can be drawn:
- The Board has contributed most in areas where college skill and resource

is most stretched: finance, property development, business planning and health & safety.

● The choice of a large Board has probably been correct. Most governors are now well involved in college matters and feel generally content with their contributions.

● Committees are all active and effective, making real decisions and contributing well to Board strategies and to executive guidance and support.

● The "representational profile" of the Board is generally satisfactory, with staff and student members making important contributions. Following the decision to form a Court for the University of Luton, with its members likely to be drawn from a geographically wider area, the more local background of Board members is probably correct. With a strong equal opportunities ethos in the institution we must continually note that we have no disabled governor and only one who comes from an ethnic minority.

● Decision-making by consensus is sought whenever possible, maintaining a unity within the Board and giving the executive the greatest possible confidence in the policies and strategies adopted.

● Briefing of governors to allow informed decisions will continue to be a challenge and, certainly, is not always fully achieved. Overall, committee briefing papers and presentations are thorough and most decisions can be well judged. At full Board meetings however, faith is needed both in the committees and the Directorate.

● New governors are better briefed and prepared, but this is still an area of concern – largely because of the rapid rate of change within the institution.

● Communications, as so often in the modern world, continue to tax the Directorate and the Board. Newsletters and circulated briefings have done much to help. Seminars will surely continue, but their timing and frequency need further examination. The decision to move to four Board meetings per year will allow a little more time for discussion, but reading and digesting all the papers will continue to be a difficult task.

● To become a governor of the new University of Luton is bound to be a fascinating and exciting challenge as well as a considerable honour.

Developing the Fabric, 1989–93

KEITH COOK

THE DECISION in 1989 to pursue polytechnic status for Luton College – which soon had to be transformed into a quest for university status – raised obvious questions about the institution's size and curriculum mix. Once the target had been clearly identified, the framework and rules of engagement were clear. As far as buildings and property were concerned the issues were perhaps less clear. Certainly if they were identified, the way of tackling them was not so obvious.

In 1989, though not without controversy, the college inherited a set of buildings on three main sites: Park Square, Dallow Road, and Putteridge Bury. The Park Square building had been constructed in the late 1950s and included a number of large single-storey craft and engineering workshops. The site in Dallow Road was originally a Victorian primary school. Putteridge Bury was a neo-Elizabethan country house in magnificent grounds which had housed the Putteridge Bury College of Education between 1966 and 1978 after which it had become Luton College's Centre for Management Studies.

How these could be moulded into a coherent whole was a relatively small problem compared with the inherited financial deficit. To achieve polytechnic status required first a rapid increase in student numbers, which would lead to increased income, some of which could be invested in the estate. However, greater numbers necessitated the construction of additional purpose-built space, which required a not insignificant lead-in period. More students also meant larger group sizes and larger spaces for teaching. Curriculum changes, in range, breadth and form of delivery, also required a remodelling of existing areas.

There was too the question of the quality and appearance of the college's properties, particularly at Park Square. The college occupied a prominent town centre site adjacent to the magnificent St Mary's Church, Luton's only remaining Grade 1 listed building. The shift from technical and further education to higher education required an accompanying change in the physical environment, and a recognition of a move into the national and international arena. Long-established universities and polytechnics could offer accommodation in purpose-built residences for hundreds, and in some cases thousands, of students. In 1989 Luton College of Higher Education had only 102 student bedspaces.

Faced with such a daunting challenge, alongside all the others, the starting point was to ask how it could be achieved and by what means. A strategy was clearly needed. In any case, the Polytechnics and Colleges Funding Council (PCFC) required an approved accommodation strategy before it would even consider awarding major capital funds. The college itself had no staff who could develop or implement such a strategy.

A two-pronged approach was adopted. Selected architects were commissioned to prepare an outline development design for Park Square with a 10-year horizon, and consultants appointed to develop a formal accommodation strategy for the whole college.

Bedford-based Charter Partnership, represented by a senior partner, John Creasey, came up with the best vision. Consultants were appointed to prepare the wider strategy.

With this process under way, other decisions had to be made. It was agreed that a priority must be a new Learning Resources Centre. An application was made to the PCFC in 1990 for funding support, but this was turned down because the accommodation strategy was not yet in place. The courageous decision was made to borrow the money and proceed anyway as clearly such a facility was a key feature of any higher education institution.

In the short term, additional leased space would have to be acquired. Fairview House on the Park Square block was leased to house Business Faculty staff, and a floor of Bank Chambers opposite for the newly formed Finance Department.

All seemed to be moving along well. In early 1991, the consultants presented the draft Accommodation Strategy, incorporating the design work of the Charter Partnership. It was accepted by the Governors as setting the framework for the way forward and sent to the PCFC, which requested a number of amendments. At about the same time the Assistant Director, Val Dempsey, decided to retire. The opportunity was taken to appoint a replacement with the key task of overseeing the strategic development of the estate and expanding the property portfolio. Keith Cook was appointed from the Polytechnic of North London with a record of similar achievements there.

Luton College had embarked on an ambitious programme of refurbishment and remodelling its existing teaching and learning accommodation. The pace was quickening on all fronts. Just before the new Assistant Director took up his post the college was successful in a bid to the PCFC minor works programme. The proposal was to convert a double volume hall into a large tiered lecture theatre and an accompanying suite of flexible teaching spaces on two floors. The show was on the road again.

The new Assistant Director was faced with two immediate tasks. The first was to recast the Accommodation Strategy so that it was acceptable to the PCFC and to get the college back into the bidding process, while simultaneously keeping existing programmes moving. The second was to put in place a strategy for increasing purpose-built student accommodation as soon as possible. These two aspects will be considered separately.

By January the Accommodation Strategy had been written and accepted by the PCFC. It covered a longer time span than the previous document and highlighted in its options the probable need for a third campus to take the strain off the town-centre site.

However, the wider aspirations of the college received a discouraging setback with the government announcement that all existing polytechnics would automatically become universities and the binary divide would disappear. Any higher education institution wanting to achieve university status would henceforth have to meet further requirements. The goalposts had been shifted just when polytechnic status was within Luton's grasp. The PCFC, which distributed the scarce capital funding, was to disappear. Nevertheless in February 1991 a bid for three phases of new building valued at some £12 million was submitted to the PCFC for consideration at its final bidding round.

In April the completed hall project and the Learning Resources Centre came on stream. At the same time, the PCFC agreed to provide £1 million towards Phase I of the major capital project. Regrettably, the council could not agree to fund further phases as it was going to be superseded by the Higher Education Funding Council for England (HEFCE).

The Charter Partnership went back to the drawing board and the college braced itself for the return of the builders, no minor event. The building work was undertaken whilst normal teaching activities continued. It is to the credit of Mariott Ltd, the contractors on the Learning Resources Centre, that this was achieved without tempers on both sides becoming frayed too often.

The summer of 1991 was a period of extreme activity. One of the existing refectories was refurbished, and reopened as The Striped Boater. Work started to create a major social facility for students in an old underground car park. This was to open six months later as The Underground, a venue with a capacity of 400. The college's main entrance was enlarged and remodelled, and a new franchised bookshop created in the old motor vehicle workshop next to the Learning Resources Centre. The former library was converted to offices and teaching space for the Health Care Faculty. Leased premises had recently been acquired for a number of activities.

First, a factory at the Hayward Tyler site had been leased and motor vehicle courses consolidated there over the summer period. A new Research Centre was established in leased premises on Crawley Green Road, owned by Measurement Technology Ltd. Finally, a new Humanities Faculty spawned by the Business Faculty needed accommodation. This was found in the former *Luton News* office and printing works in Castle Street. Major conversion works were undertaken in a matter of months because the existing lessor went into liquidation on the day contracts were to be signed. Anxious months were spent "squatting" until a new lease was signed with the owners at Christmas 1991.

Meanwhile, delicate negotiations were under way with the Borough Council, St Mary's Church and English Heritage regarding Phase I of the major project. This project envisaged constructing additional floors on two flat roofs on the buildings at Park Square, and an additional two floors on the Vicarage Street building. Because of the visual impact on St Mary's Church, planning permission for the latter was initially refused. The project was then split in two and work started on the Park Square rooftops. This project was dogged with misfortune from the start, with major water ingress to the floors below disrupting normal working activities over several months.

It was decided to submit amended plans for the Vicarage Street building. These pushed the overall cost of the project up from £2 million to £2.5 million. However, several positive things emerged from this debacle. Planning permission was given for an additional single floor over the whole building, including the newly proposed three-storey extension. The refectory was refurbished at the same time and reopened as The Pavilion. English Heritage gave support for the wider development proposals at Park Square on the grounds that they would greatly enhance the visual relationship between St Mary's Church and the existing college buildings.

The 1992–93 academic year was a difficult one, with the building works having a far greater impact than anyone had anticipated. However, this did not detract from the achievement of taught degree awarding powers, followed shortly after by research degree awarding powers and university status in July 1993. The two rooftop projects were completed behind schedule but just in time to open for the start of the 1993–94 academic year. The student enrolment in the autumn of 1993 was the first to take place under the institution's new title of the University of Luton. It was a bumper recruitment, emphasising the importance of the planned building programme continuing to completion. Further targets for the immediate future were to include:

● a revised Accommodation Strategy which would take into account the increased student population figures;

● the need to seek further leased property for teaching purposes on a short-term basis;

• a reduction in the intensity of the traditional summer programme of building refurbishment, in favour of a more considered rolling maintenance programme;

• early planning for the possible development of a third campus and science park at Butterfield Green on the boundary of the town.

The provision of good-quality residential accommodation for students also represented a considerable challenge, in view of the fact that the institution had no funds or access to public funds, and no land on which to build. The policy framework was established in 1991, to move from the existing 112 bedspaces to a position where every first-year full-time student from outside the locality could be offered a place in purpose-built accommodation. Until this could be achieved, the college's head tenancy scheme (managed rented accommodation) and the private sector would have to take much of the strain.

The intention was to establish all building programmes on a self-financing basis, with costs being recovered through the rental income charged to students. The route to this would be to use private developers and private funding.

As a start, the college raised a loan and purchased 23 houses in Luton, which converted to 92 bedspaces for the 1992 intake. A year later, a further 500 bedspaces were added through the construction of new, purpose-built accommodation, in schemes adjoining Biscot Road, Hibbert Street, John Street, and Guildford Street. The process was set to accelerate rapidly during 1993–94 with the building of a further 1,000 bedspaces for completion in September 1994. All such schemes represent good examples of what can be achieved through close cooperation between the public and private sectors.

The development of an appropriate property portfolio for the new university has not been easy, and this pattern is unlikely to change in the future. Financial resources have always been tight, and it has been necessary to reinvest most surpluses to achieve the advances sought. However, determination has overcome the many hardships, setbacks and disappointments encountered along the way, and there is confidence this same commitment will carry us forward successfully in the future.

An Administrator
Looks Back

PAM VACHON

MY ASSOCIATION with the institution now known as the University of Luton spans four decades. As a student in the last year of the 1950s I could sit in class and watch the shire horses leave Flower's Breweries from Park Street West to deliver their loads. We shared our Business Studies classes with trainee managers from Vauxhall Motors, "cub" journalists from the Luton News and staff from many of the other major employers in the town.

There are others, much better informed than me, who will have provided some of the facts, figures and dates about the creation of the university. As a Lutonian, to me the institution which has been on this site all of my life has been at the heart of the town. Most of my family have at some time been students at it.

When I joined the staff of what was then Luton College of Technology in 1964 the largest departments were Engineering and Food & Fashion. The building was full of apprentices in overalls and trainee chefs in tall white hats. At that time Luton was synonymous with Vauxhall Motors, all of whose apprentices had to do a day-release course at "The Tec".

The whole administrative staff fitted in one large room. Some 12 in number, we spent a good part of our days selling graph paper at eight sheets for 1d and exercise books at 3d each. There were no computers to assist us in preparing returns for the Department of Education & Science – Sinclair had not even invented the pocket calculator yet. All records were kept on cards, which we counted in various ways to arrive at official returns and all the other statistics required.

The top of the clerical salary scale was £725 per annum. This was recognised when the annual dinner and dance at the George Hotel, the highlight of the college's social calendar, came round. Administrative staff were admitted at half price because it was felt they could not afford the full £3!

A HATFUL OF TALENT

It was a strange world to me then, with its endless discussions about whether Luton or Hatfield would achieve polytechnic status and whether an external University of London degree in engineering would be approved. Luton lost out in both cases.

Apart from a full-time Higher National Diploma course in engineering, whose students were almost exclusively employees of General Motors, the higher education courses were all part-time day release. Most of the full-time students were in further education, training to be hairdressers, chefs and secretaries or taking GCE A levels.

There were few demarcation lines. I had a special responsibility for work required by the Principal, but the title Secretary or Assistant was never used. We were all either clerical assistants or clerical officers. We dealt with correspondence, collected fees, checked registers, prepared reports and examination papers, and acted as examination invigilators. The memories of invigilating examinations in the Art School on hot Saturday afternoons in mid-summer are still vivid. The constant fear was of nodding off – the heat coming through the mainly glass building rivalled a glasshouse at Kew Gardens.

As the 1960s merged into the 1970s changes were afoot. The Vicarage Street building had been approved and built. Known at the beginning as the "Feeder College", nobody seemed quite sure to what use it was to be put. Then more transformations – with the closing of the Technical School, Barnfield College of Further Education was opened and the Department of Food & Fashion and the Schools of Art and Secretarial Studies were transferred from Park Square to the new institution.

The administrative section of the college underwent rapid change. The "omnibus" office disappeared to be replaced by departmental secretaries and assistants – from jacks-of-all-trades we started to become specialists.

The 1970s also saw the introduction of a computerised student record system. Oh the expectations! No more counting of thousands of cards; we had only to press a button and all would be revealed. The first attempt yielded one male student under 21 in the whole college. Back to the cards!

Then came another government White (or was it Green?) Paper and Luton College of Technology set about becoming Luton College of Higher Education. The Putteridge Bury College of Education became a part of the new institution but all too soon the Education part left again. It was a traumatic period for many of the staff. It soon became apparent to us all that this was not the end of change, rather the beginning.

With the announcement of government proposals for higher education in the 1980s, Luton College found itself at the crossroads.

114

Always in the top 10 of higher education institutions in the country, even in those days the college had a national reputation for excellence, but the transition from omnibus college still had to take place. The composition of the student body had already changed considerably. Full-time degree and Higher National Diploma courses now accounted for more than half of the work. But would it be enough to enable Luton College to ensure its national position?

The college's decision to seek independence from local education authority control began the most taxing and demanding period, one of unrivalled activity. The commitment and dedication of those responsible for the future of the institution inspired all the staff. It was a nerve-wracking period as first one hurdle was cleared only for another to rear up ahead. The position was finally made clear in November 1988 – a telephone call while I was spending a few days in North Wales gave me the news we had all been awaiting. We had four months to prepare for our independence on 1 April 1989.

But yet again it was not the end of the story, merely another beginning. We entered our new existence with some 500 full-time higher education students. We were not aware of it but already the vision of the University of Luton was taking form.

The administrative structure now had to cope with the responsibilities of a self-governing institution. Financial and personnel functions had to be in place. Looking back now it seems impossible that so much was accomplished in such a short time. The institution had always operated as a team, and never was this more necessary than now.

The dream was finally realised on 14 July 1993 when university status was achieved. The foundations had been laid many years before. The administrative staff, in particular, had been required to adapt to many changes. This they had done with goodwill and enthusiasm.

The University of Luton is a success story. Its success shows that people of vision can accomplish the seemingly impossible if their belief is strong enough. I look back over the past 30 years with great pleasure. It has never been less than completely absorbing. To tell the truth the storms were no less enjoyable than the calms. The end result was well worth it all. ■

Learning Resources: A Brief History

ALAN GEESON

Before Luton College's Park Square building was constructed in 1957 any library provision was extremely rudimentary and provided by the Borough of Luton Public Library, one of the foremost and most progressive public libraries in the UK under the leadership of Frank Gardner. The building was originally envisaged as very much a small local college just to serve local business and industry. Symptomatic of the rivalry between the Bedfordshire County Council and the rapidly growing and prosperous Borough of Luton, the county's proposals were completely inadequate in size and quality and the Ministry of Education, which had recognised the value of libraries in colleges of further education, insisted on better standards, including a library. This originally occupied the second-floor bridge area and only the bridge. The Minister was soon proved right, as a second building had to be built within a few years in Vicarage Street which included a library in its original design. This was the ground-floor room known as the goldfish bowl, which was never used for library purposes. Even then the college was bulging at the seams, with teaching in corridors and various old hat factories and schools.

The new library on the bridge was furnished with wooden furniture of excellent quality, some of it still in use in the new resource centre. Shelving was of mahogany with brass fittings, tables were solidly made and initially chairs were wooden in a Windsor style. A small periodicals room and a tiny Librarian's office were included. There was a store/workroom without natural light or ventilation, hardly fit for human beings to work in.

The college was fortunate in its first Librarian, Ian Rogerson, who came as one of the new breed of active young professional librarians from the new library schools. He was very active in the profession and has just retired from a chair at Manchester Metropolitan University. Ian was good at public relations and set about vigorously getting the service started and accepted. As he had only one assistant, this meant long hours simply covering the counter for them both. The climate in those days was very different. The Science Department was preparing students for the London External BSc and was one of the three most successful in the country. It also did many specialised high-level courses for industry and fairly early on began to do research. Mechanical Engineering also offered degree-level work and made heavy demands for journal articles and research papers, and the School of Art used the library as a source for illustrations. The other departments concentrated on lower-level work, mainly part-time, for industry, and on GCE A and O levels. Laboratory and workshop-based work predominated.

Most of the teaching staff had come up the hard route through apprenticeship and night school and many years of part-time slog and were essentially practical people who saw no need for an "academic" library. In most cases they were working to syllabuses set by outside bodies for which set texts were available. In the 1960s liberal studies became a necessary but unpopular part of City &Guilds and National Certificate and Diploma courses. In most colleges the liberal studies department was seen as a natural ally of the library service but not at Luton.

A good foundation had been laid by Ian Rogerson and he was succeeded by Mr Lawrence who organised the library systems soundly and laid the basis of the cataloguing and issue systems used up to automation before he moved to Preston Polytechnic. He was followed by Alan Tyson who moved to public libraries in the North East.

At this time the College of Technology was under the County Borough of Luton and its Director of Education, Dr J. H. Corbett, who had a difficult task trying to design a good education system entirely different from that of the county, cooperation with which was frowned on. The college worked very closely with the Town Hall and most of the administration was done at the Education Offices or Borough Treasurer's department.

The library at this period had grown slowly with two additional rooms,including a separate study room for smokers. In 1969 Alan Geeson was appointed College Librarian, the first Librarian to be appointed on teaching scales as a lecturer I, but initially he had no involvement in decision-making, being directly responsible to the Principal, Dr Roy Steed, who did his best to support the service from very limited resources and close control from the Borough. Indicative of this was the insistence that the library should stocktake annually, no mean job for two staff, and one not imposed on the public library. It added nothing to student learning but was typical of meddling from outsiders who did not understand education at that time.

In 1969 the staffing was one librarian, and one full-time and one part-time assistant. The book fund was £4,000 and the provision was mainly books and journals, with a full set of British Standards for the Engineers and Builders, an illustration collection and little else. The library was typical of many of the larger colleges of the period but always tried to be forward-looking. For example, it acquired early on a curious photocopier, the first in the college, which had to be filled weekly with a noxious fluid, and a microfilm and microfiche reader at a very early date.

In 1970 the Department of Education & Science published DES Circular 7/70, which proposed the development of a much more democratic form of college government with elected staff members on an academic board which also had the college librarian as an ex-officio member. There was a fine balance between the heads of department and elected members – the unions saw this as an opportunity and the management as a threat – and college librarians suddenly found themselves courted by both sides. At Luton the Librarian was promptly invited to join the heads of department group and eventually found himself serving on far too many of the rapidly growing sub-committees and working parties arising from the Academic Board. These developments did much to raise the profile of libraries but for us the period of expansion was just around the corner.

London University announced that it was stopping the granting of external degrees in science, the college's most successful area of work, and gloom descended. Fortunately for Luton College, however, as a result of a very strong fight by all concerned it won the right to offer CNAA degrees. The effect on the Library was immediate – the CNAA was a powerful force for improvement in standards and staffing, and book fund and accommodation soon began to increase to meet its requirements although it was a hard fight with much opposition from some departments within the college.

Joan Gallop was appointed as the first Tutor/Librarian in Bedfordshire to increase the amount and quality of library tuition to students, and more non-professional staff were added, Mrs Paddy Greig and Mrs Audrey Burton being two of those appointed then who gave long and excellent service.

The book fund rose steadily, as did stock and journal holdings. Audiotapes and video tapes became available and Teletext and Prestel were provided. Improved photocopying machines appeared and accommodation grew piecemeal, another room being added before several CNAA visits in spite of opposition from some departments. Single study carrels were bought and the change to more internally designed courses and assignment-based learning led to a heavy increase in the use of the request service and a steady growth in book issues. We began to feel the increase of student demand for seating and other facilities which had steadily grown to create overwhelming pressure, leading to overcrowding and noise problems. The college was a very heavy user of the British Library at Boston Spa, being one of the first to access this service by telex, and was a founder member of the Bedfordshire Libraries and Information Group. We put in the first bid in Bedfordshire for a book-loss detection system but unfortunately were less successful in gaining the capital for an automated library system – this did not come until the late 1980s.

The CNAA was the motivating force for these improvements and the first visit by Ken Garside, Goldsmiths' College's Librarian, and later visits, notably one by Peter Pack of Edgehill representing the CNAA, put considerable pressure on the college and the LEA. Pressure was also coming from a more articulate student body, the emphasis of whose work was changing away from science and engineering courses with a laboratory or workshop basis towards business studies work. These students needed much better periodical and statistical provision. In the late 1970s study packs were started and the library was an early user of the new on-line information services which have done so much to improve access to current information.

In 1986 capital was at last obtained to make a start on library automation and a CALM system running on a Novell network of PCs was acquired which enabled work to start on cataloguing. Fortunately, money later became available to upgrade to the proven LIBERTAS system in 1990, which has proved an excellent investment.

In the 1970s and early 1980s the college had a hard fight to maintain its position and proportion of high-level work but eventually gained independence from LEA control, which led to accelerated growth of higher-level work, more demands on learning resources, provision for new subjects such as the expensive law area and the planning and design of the new Learning Resources Centre on the site of what was previously engineering workshops. Mr Geeson retired in 1989 to be replaced by Tim Stone, now part of the management team of Learning Resources, which was formed by combining the Libraries, Computer Services and Communication Services of the University of Luton under Richard Walker. The well-designed and generously equipped new centre was formally opened in 1993 and is becoming busier, better supported and more heavily used day by day to the point where it is almost overwhelmed by its own success and already shows the need for expansion.

While this steady growth was taking place at Park Square the old College of Education at Putteridge Bury, a day college for mature trainee teachers, had gradually built up a much more "academic" type of library in the ballroom, now the main conference room. This was a very traditional library, making provision for teaching practice and having a good collection in education and English literature. Furnishing was of the utilitarian Remploy softwood range, but the room was delightful with its high ceiling and plasterwork, outlook over the gardens and peaceful atmosphere. Joseph Magoon, a librarian and bookman of the old school, who would take endless trouble for any of his students, reigned there for many years with very little help. The pattern of use was very uneven, with busy spells as teaching practice started and finished and very quiet periods between.

In the 1970s there was a cutback in teacher training and many small colleges were closed, and in 1976 Putteridge Bury merged with Luton College of Technology to form Luton College of Higher Education. Much of Putteridge Bury's collection was dispersed and Putteridge Bury became a centre for management courses, the library coming under the control of Mr Geeson, now Head of Library Services for the College of Higher Education. When Dr Tony Wood became Director, the role of Putteridge Bury was reviewed and a conference centre was developed which included the Putteridge Bury Library. A resource centre was set up in the old gymnasium, which included about 40 microcomputers with access to the Luton College mainframe system, a small TV studio and a teaching room which proved very successful to the point where the demand outgrew the space such that separate computer suites were set up in the college.

The College's first taste of computing was provided by the County Borough of Luton in about 1969 when it insisted on the use of the Town Hall mainframe for financial control. This was a disaster, errors usually being of the order of 200–300 per cent, and it set back the development of administrative computing for many years. In the early 1970s a small mainframe with a terminal room and links to high schools and other local colleges was installed for teaching purposes. At that time, computing was viewed as an adjunct of mathematics and was under the control of the Maths Department where it was treated with suspicion by many of the teaching staff and the Head of Department. The new centre soon became independent under Mike Williams and later John Marshall, both of whom were keen to expand and develop its role. In the 1970s departments were coerced reluctantly into exposing their students to what many regarded as a new toy but changes in technology, the development of microcomputers, better staffing and provision, involvement of teaching staff and the vision of a few farsighted members of the college, including Dr Steed, led to the growth to the present situation. There are now 25 or so specialist computer staff, an excellent modern computer centre, technical support, computer suites throughout the university (many networked), and links to outside bodies. There is provision for all students to have generous access in the expectation that they will make full use of the technology available.

The enthusiasm of two members of the teaching staff, Roy Stares and Doug Withey, together with the support of the then vice-principal, Peter Rossington, and a small band of teaching staff who could see the potential benefits of the adoption of educational technology and new teaching methods, led to the development of what was initially a facility for recording and playing back off-air recordings of BBC and ITV programmes and a studio for the making of in-house programmes. Many rooms were wired so that TV programmes could be used in teaching, and a vigorous policy of keeping up to date with changes in technology and close involvement with the Educational Television Association, together with staff development, has kept the university in the forefront in the use of television and educational technology.

The university has started with a new £3.2 million resources centre with 120,000 volumes, 850 periodical titles, films, videos, CD ROMs, opportunity to access information on-line worldwide and good provision of study places. This is complemented by a smaller resource centre at Putteridge Bury.

The resources centre has holdings of 1,500 recorded TV programmes for class use, there are extensive facilities for programme production and recording, and very generous provision is made of computer facilities at varying levels as appropriate for users throughout the university.

All of this is a vast development from the situation when Ian Rogerson and his single assistant were fighting for recognition and support from one room on the bridge 33 years ago, and reflects the changes in technology and in teaching, particularly the level and range of subject taught, and the methods used. Mainly, however, it is the result of a great deal of hard work, commitment and thought by those involved in the provision and the support given to learning resources by successive college authorities.

Field Courses

JOHN HASSELL

IT HAS LONG been accepted that the incorporation of field courses into curricula is almost certain to improve the educational experience of students, enriching their studies. Field trips have been undertaken for more than 25 years, in the vast majority of cases very successfully, by most departments and faculties at Luton. This chapter tries to give a flavour of their value for students, staff and the institution, and to reflect students' opinions of the courses. Lack of time and space precludes a detailed look at all types of field courses but a Built Environment trip serves as one example.

It was 6.30am on a cold Sunday morning in early February 1993. Bleary-eyed students began to assemble on the Park Square car park looking distinctly uninterested. The joviality of the member of staff organising things did nothing to improve the humour of the students – indeed, as 7am approached, accompanied by rain, their resentment grew. They all hated him at this moment anyway. Why were they all here? Why didn't he drown himself or something?

By 7am only a couple of students were missing, the other staff members had arrived and the mini-convoy was preparing to leave. The laggards then arrived, dragging rucksacks behind them as two mini-buses and a luggage van started up. The only things that looked sadder than the students were the aforementioned rucksacks, tied to equally sad-looking pairs of boots and sleeping bags covered in black plastic refuse sacks. To no-one's surprise within 10 minutes the mini-buses became mobile dormitories in spite of the unreasonable behaviour of a jovial person who seemed to think himself a bit of a singer.

Six-and-a-half hours later the centre at Hartsop, near Glenridding in the Lake District, was reached and chaos reigned for half an hour as the students asserted maximum effort to obtain the best beds, and minimum effort in unloading provisions. Whilst the staff were remarking to each other how much students in their early to mid-twenties reminded them of their children in their early teens, the students were telling each other how like their parents the staff were.

Much to everyone's surprise, the majority of us slept most of the night. It was a good thing we did. Day two brought Lake District rain at its best: horizontal, stinging and very cold. The day was taken up with an ascent of a mountain named High Street – so-called because of the Roman Road which crosses it. Visibility varied from not much to even less, and it was soon obvious why waterproofs were required. After two hours most boots had become waterlogged and breakfast had long been forgotten. Two less fit and less than ideally equipped students were sent back to the centre but everyone else plodded on. The walk was unremittingly upwards while the rain was just simply unremitting. The summit was reached after four hours and after a stop only long enough to consume packed lunches the descent was begun in even harder rain that was turning to sleet.

Unfortunately it never turned to snow, which is much more pleasant. Seven hours after leaving the centre, as darkness falls, the centre was reached. Hot soup, rolls, tea, and showers somehow miraculously turned feelings of dejection into a wholesome sense of achievement. Later still a superb casserole (cooked by the nut-jobs who had dragged the students up the mountain) increased the sense of well-being even more. Even a lecture on first aid failed to dim entirely a new-found interest in, at least, hill-walking.

Day three saw further previously dismissed activities being sampled and, by and large, enjoyed. Not everyone enjoyed abseiling but those who didn't enjoyed the orienteering, and vice-versa. Even the rain, not in the mood to go elsewhere, failed to discourage anyone and a good portion of the time, during the second visit to the pub, was spent discussing the various merits of the activities sampled so far. It was remarked amongst the staff that in the space of only three days the students had matured quite considerably. A topic of conversation amongst the students was the way in which the staff had changed in such a short time.

Day four was gorge-scrambling day. In this instance the rain was absolutely no problem at all since it is almost inevitable that one gets wet when gorge-scrambling. The object is to walk up a river gorge, keeping to rocks in the river or clinging to the sides of the gorge when there are no rocks to step on, for as long and as far as one can. With the quantity of rain which had preceded and accompanied this particular field trip, the river was swollen, a whirling cauldron of white water in many places. Most of the gorge had an umbrella of trees and in parts it was somewhat subfusc, if not downright gloomy.

Within half an hour of starting, all the students had had at least one leg up to the knee in the river, and by the end of the first hour most had been thigh-deep. The water was very, very cold. Inevitably the rock-scrambling took its toll of energy, and by the time it was decided to call it a day a considerable number of students (and the writer) had fallen into the river completely.

The afternoon group fared similarly. Nevertheless the need to help each other on many occasions, the trepidation felt at the outset of the gorge walk, and the conquering of the fears, contributed to an even greater sense of achievement being experienced by all than had been gained from the earlier activities.

Back at the centre, the evening meal was followed by the considerable task of groups planning their expeditions for the following day. Map-reading, compass work, route-planning, completion of route cards, devising escape routes and walk timings took up all the evening. The forecast was for better weather.

The fifth day saw the three groups of students being blindfolded and taken by mini-buses to various points, each approximately 10 miles from the centre, in accordance with the previous night's planning. They had then to make their way back to the centre as quickly and safely as possible. Unknown to the groups the field trip manager would be out and about with binoculars checking on their progress, being joined later by the other lecturers, who had acted as taxi-drivers. All groups arrived back safely.

On their return, after food, drink and a shower, all students completed a written assessment, worked together on some management exercises, and then everyone went to the grandly named Alhambra cinema in Keswick. After the film there was still time to conclude the day with a drink or two in a previously unvisited hostelry in Keswick.

The cleaning of the centre prior to departure on the following morning was completed with an enthusiasm that had apparently been non-existent five days previously. While the students had matured beyond belief in six days (said the staff), the staff had become unrecognisable from their "predecessors" of six days earlier (said the students).

On other field trips we have experienced a "white-out" on the summit plateau of Helvellyn, all-night bivouacs at Coniston Old Man and Catalycan, being stuck in the "cheese-press" whilst caving in Yorkshire, falling into the Atlantic whilst sea-cliff traversing off Anglesey, and carrying a student all the way down Skiddaw after she was blown over the summit and badly sprained her ankle. It is highly likely that the experiences of members of staff and students from other faculties are more varied and unusual than the ones related above. I also don't doubt

125

that the value of their field courses is as great as the ones organised by my own faculty.

As the university develops and ultimately expands, it is certain that the menu of field courses will broaden. It could well be that totally free-standing field courses may be developed into a major source of income for the institution. It is certainly the case that courses of the summer-school type will be the only occasion that all students on a number of courses come together, the remainder of their education being carried out on a distant-learning basis. Whatever their form, field trips will remain: they are among the things that keep us sane. ■

Library Staff, Christmas 1981

Library Rounders Team, June 1984

Mobile Roadshow, 1987

Flexibus, 1988

Luton College of Higher Education Academic Board, March 1989

Standing (left to right): A Euinton, P Hewitt, J Marshall, M Daniel, M Fulton, T Rhodes, S Mortimer, A Evesham, J Moss Jones, R Driver, D Millward, D Curren, C Westwood, K Bentley, A Geeson, B Roe, P Raffles, I Southam
Seated (left to right): W Aitken, V Dempsey, J Clarke, L Hughes, A J Wood, F Howarth, C Fernandes, S Kowalczuk

Great Putteridge Bury Garden Party, 15 July 1993

Great Putteridge Bury Garden Party, 15 July 1993

Great Putteridge Bury Garden Party, 15 July 1993

Grand Celebration Ball, 16 July 1993

Putteridge Bury from the air

University Academic Board, 2 December 1993

From left to right: (back) B Roe, R Walker, P Gray, T Stone, R Harris, R Driver, Dr C Larrea

(middle) K Yousaf, D Bedward, D Wickens, C Osborn, Professor D Rawson, T Boatswain, B Lehaney, Professor P Birch, Professor K Robinson, C Eccles, D Brown

(front) C Harris, Dr L Dunkley, Dr D John (Vice Chairman), Dr A J Wood (Chairman), B Bell, J Dolan

Absent: K Cook, S Mortimer, P Beagle

First meeting of the University Board of Governors at Putteridge Bury, 4 November 1993

Present (clockwise from left-hand corner): A Dongworth, A Higginson, D Ludlow, Rt Rev. D Farmbrough, J Bonner, G Slessor, B Howseman, J Drage, I Greenwood, County Cllr J Thakoordin, Dr T Whitear, D Palmer, E Stephens, S Cuthbertson, P Henman, Cllr L Collier, T Lines (Vice Chancellor), Dr A J Wood (Vice Chancellor), Professor J Matthews (Chairman), P Grayson (Clerk), A Burton (Secretary) Others present (back left to right): K Cook, R Harris, B Roe, R Combes, R Jeyes, I Nicol, D Bedward, Professor D Rawson, Dr D John, Professor K Robinson, F Howarth, R Williams

Inauguration of the University, 26 November 1993. From left to right: Dr Tony Wood (Vice Chancellor), Sir David Plastow (Chancellor) and Professor John Matthews (Chairman of Governors and Pro-Chancellor)

**Inauguration of the University of Luton, 26 November 1993
at the Parish Church of St Mary's**

Four Honorary Fellows (left to right): Dr Roy Steed, Frank Lester OBE, Kelvin Hopkins, Graham Bright MP

Graduation ceremonies, 1993

Emiko Asada, 25, Japan, and Christine Barbe, 23, France. English for Overseas Students. Emiko: "Studying the culture is as interesting as the language." Christine: "I now aim to work for the European Community."

Vincent Lattimore, 22, Tipperary. MSc Decision Making. "This programme was ideal. There are no more than 15 students in any one class. I am really enjoying the course, it is very challenging."

Claire Perrin, 19, Torquay. BA Pyschology & Women's Studies. "My course is so innovative and we cover a wide spectrum of ideas and theories. It has opened the door to a variety of careers."

Rebecca Stafford-Jones, 19, South Wales. BSc (Hons) Building Surveying."The sandwich element of the course appealed to me – I can't wait to get out there and into the working environment."

Students' views of the University

Commemorative University Items, 1993

University of Luton Reception, 1993

Marketing Higher Education at Luton

CRAIG MATHIESON

ARKETING is like an iceberg: what is seen on top belies the structure beneath. However, successful marketing requires a clear understanding of infrastructure, and marketing education is about working with people and for people. Managing change, and introducing the marketing philosophy, is where Luton College's marketing programme began.

Background

The 1988 Education Reform Act was a watershed for British education. Through the legislation, the Department of Education & Science acquired new powers in relation to curriculum, schemes for financial delegation and the approval of grant-maintained school applications. At the same time, local education authorities (LEAs) lost much of their day-to-day control of some schools and higher education colleges, as power was devolved to these institutions. With such major changes under way, it was perhaps not surprising for claims to be made that this was the most important piece of educational legislation since the Second World War.

The new responsibilities imposed on higher education colleges placed a premium on effective management. Principals, directors and senior staff, formerly entrusted with, trained in, and with experience of curriculum and pedagogy, found themselves having to acquire new skills in staff management, finance and marketing. Such skills were seen as necessary for them to lead their institutions into a new competitive era.

These were important issues in relation to the developments that took place in Luton College during this period. For the belief that began to emerge from the legislation was that "educational management was to be concerned with the internal operation of educational institutions, and with their relationships within the environments and communities in which they operated, in addition to the government bodies to which they were now formally responsible". College leaders were seen as having a key role to play in formulating the aims and goals of their institutions.

Certainly, in what was then Luton College of Higher Education, the marketing function emerged from strong and positive support from the directorate and senior staff for the principle of developing a culture built on the perceived needs of the market.

Examination of the 1988 Education Reform Act will identify key words current in the 1980s. These include "responsiveness", a "market-oriented approach", "choice", "customer satisfaction" and "competition". Such notions have pervaded government policies for the last decade. Evident throughout the Act is a stress on educational institutions responding to the needs of students and servicing the needs of employers as primary and secondary clients, with autonomy and freedom being given to institutions to compete against each other in the marketplace.

This concept has never been seriously challenged. The key controversies have been about the groups to which the services ought to be most responsive, about how they should demonstrate this responsiveness, and who might legitimately define the needs of client groups.

A view prevailed for many years that the professionals within the education services, such as LEA officers, were best placed to address such matters. The 1988 Education Reform Act dealt a major blow to this viewpoint. Powers, along with responsibilities, were moved to central government and lay governing bodies. More important, the Act gave autonomy, within guidelines, to education institutions to develop their own destinies in the development of educational programmes and their delivery.

Even before the 1988 legislation, further and higher education institutions had been urged to improve their marketing, through such White Papers as *Training for Jobs* (DES/DE, 1984) and *Higher Education: Meeting the Challenge* (DES, 1987), and the 1985 Audit Commission report. So it is perhaps not surprising that Luton College, along with many others in the sector, had begun to appoint individuals with responsibilities for marketing.

There was, however, a major difference between Luton's approach and that of many other institutions. Most made their first appointments at a relatively junior level with allocated timetables which permitted three to four hours a week to be devoted to marketing services as part of a job that included other responsibilities. By contrast, from the outset Luton College positioned marketing at a senior management level. This, along with the supporting marketing infrastructure of staffing and budgets, set Luton's structure apart from those of many of its peers at the time.

Mission
The basic principle of marketing derives from the practice of marketing industrial products and consumer durables. Industrial and commercial

businesses need to develop a rational sequence of activities. Thus an organisation identifies the need to market a new product, or improve the marketing of one that is declining or causing problems.

The process evolves around an audit and includes the identification of market segments and their characteristics, and research into the preferences and expectations of a sample of those segments. Thus one explores opportunities in new and existing markets. On the basis of such evidence, a plan is derived which describes selected target markets and predicted demand rates.

This operational application is based on the concept of a "marketing mix", with each element of the mix being considered in turn in order to achieve an effective balance. The organisation then implements the marketing plan through agreed strategies and tactics.

At the point of independence from LEA control on 1 April 1989, the mission and objectives of Luton College underwent major review, resulting in substantial changes, both to the internal structure and to the course portfolio. The latter was adjusted to meet better the perceived needs of students and clients. Such an approach does not, however, command universal acceptance by educationalists. It is perceived by many as treating education services as if they are tangible products. A number of the staff at Luton had similar reservations, but the principle was strongly carried forward by the directorate and governors and has, in the event, been instrumental to the subsequent success enjoyed by the college and university.

To the classical "four Ps" of marketing – product, place, price and promotion – were added the three of people, process management and physical evidence. The people dimension has proven to be particularly important, for in the education business the service is very dependent on the staff who deliver that service. They need to know, understand, and take ownership of the corporate mission and objectives, if success is to be attained.

Commitment

Once marketing was established as being an important management function, the next stage was to demonstrate to the staff – our "internal customers" – how our traditions and strengths could be used to market the college. The intention was to help them understand that they had a vital and continuing role to play in this process, and that only with their help could we succeed in creating favourable perceptions of the organisation among prospective students and clients. There was also a wider task to address: to ensure our concern to satisfy the present customers was seen as an investment for the future not just an expedient for the present.

Perhaps for the first time, staff not directly involved in teaching began to realise they too had an important role to play in shaping the future. However good the quality of teaching might be, the college's reputation would be permanently damaged if low standards were practised by supporting staff like receptionists, telephonists, technicians, cleaners, caterers and secretaries.

An institution-wide programme entitled Quality Network was introduced, based around the principle of Total Quality Management, in which mixed groups of staff considered and debated the beliefs and values underpinning the college's mission. Quality Circles were established to focus on defined areas. The aim was to show the interdependency of staff, to build mutual respect and confidence, and to demonstrate the value and importance of every job undertaken in the college. All were equally vital to our long-term success.

From such activities grew a heightened awareness of the importance of staff development and skills training, which led to the introduction of an annual Career Review scheme, and to the eventual achievement, during the first year of existence of the University of Luton, of the prestigious Investor in People award administered by the Technician and Education Councils on behalf of HM Government – the first university in the country to gain this recognition.

Achieving strategic goals

A major strength of the college and university has been the ability to recognise external change, and introduce new activities for which there appears to be a demand. Market research has therefore been an important function of the work of the Marketing Unit. The introduction of many successful fields of study testifies to this approach. In the early 1990s a growing demand for more flexibility and choice in study patterns and subjects was correctly anticipated, leading to the introduction in 1993 of one of the largest and most comprehensive modular schemes in the country.

The new modular programme exemplifies one particular outcome of the general approach adopted over the period 1989–93. When it was decided at the beginning of this period that the college should aim to become a polytechnic within three years, it was clear that effective marketing would be crucial, in particular to ensure three specific goals were attained. First, to achieve a higher profile for the college in the marketplace, with wider recognition of the quality and range of study programmes. Second, to engender an understanding among prospective clients that the institution was a responsive one, and would listen to, and be prepared to act upon, their expressed needs. Third – a specific requirement for polytechnic status – to recruit significant numbers of full-time higher education students, especially at undergraduate/postgraduate levels.

To achieve these targets, the Marketing Unit first directed its efforts to the internal and external image projected by the college. All printed matter was scrutinised, to ensure a clear and consistent message in terms of appearance, purpose, style, and quality. Internal communication networks were reviewed, with publications being automatically routed through the Unit. Advertisements were related closely in format to the comparable published material, and publication scheduled through the year to coincide with key recruitment cycles. All these measures soon had a very positive effect.

Simultaneously, substantial resources were invested in developing personal contacts with individuals well placed to influence prospective students. Teachers, careers officers, further education college staff and company training officers represented important groups in this regard. Alongside this was a drive to introduce the college to overseas audiences through the British Council network, and to become better known to that body's officers.

Marketing quickly became a high-profile activity. The final significant element in this was to increase the college's direct exposure to prospective students through attendance at careers and education fairs. In 1989, 12 such events were attended; in 1993 this had risen to 295, of which many were repeat invitations to attend venues at which particularly constructive relationships had been developed with the organising body. Current evidence suggests that, regardless of the route by which they were recruited, the majority of new students have at some stage visited the college's (now university's) stand at one of these conventions.

Conclusions

The approach to marketing at Luton has been structured and customer-driven. It has been heavily dependent on staff involvement, and their individual recognition that each has a part to play. Important characteristics have been:

- establishing key objectives which are widely understood, and systematically collecting market research data;
- developing a rolling and costed marketing plan to help deliver overall college strategy; and
- implementing the plan, and continuously evaluating its success in meeting institutional goals.

Many universities and colleges choose not to adopt such a systematic approach, although the signs are that some of these may have to change their strategy in the future if they wish to remain competitive. It is unlikely the former college at Luton could have grown into a university within the relatively short window of opportunity made available by the government in any other way.

A HATFUL OF TALENT

While the new university's future needs will inevitably vary from those of the past, it is unlikely that the general principles which have driven marketing at Luton, and which have served the institution so well, will change significantly in the years immediately ahead.

Don's Diary

GERALD VINTEN

FRIDAY. *Make first visit as an assessor for the Higher Education Funding Council in business and management. Frenetic pace with meetings and lectures to attend every second of the day, plus trying to cope with campus layout designed to disorientate the newcomer. Surprisingly manage to fit it all in, and return home to the Barbican in time to see* Farewell My Concubine. *On way back pass a shop which displays a sign: "Keep up the flogging until morale improves". Wonder if any university would adopt this as its motto.*

SATURDAY/SUNDAY. *Begin to write the factual part of assessors' report, and formulate questions to explore on days two and three of visit.*

MONDAY. *Continue the assessment visit. On Monday's underground journey change trains at King's Cross. Typically the usual platform entrance is barred. Subsequent enquiry reveals that the staff do not know why. Miss the next train. Perhaps worth it to capture the immortal words of the man emerging from the train now pulling out of the opposite platform. Gently merry with intoxication, he helpfully advises: "You've just missed that train. And you've missed the other one too."*

TUESDAY. *Whitbread Literary Award at the Porter Tun Room of the old Chiswell Street Brewery, now a conference and business venue. Meet Dr Tony Whitear, R and D director, and my link person at the company, and receive introductions to Sam Whitbread and senior directors. Pleasant table of literary critics, novelists, TV personalities – and a potential novelist – me. Avoid mentioning my ambitions in order to avoid the standard response – don't talk about it like everybody else; go and do it.*

Professor Gerald Vinten's "Don's Diary" first appeared in the *Times Higher Education Supplement* of 18 February 1994. It is reproduced here with the kind permission of the author and the *THES*.

A HATFUL OF TALENT

May I have a sabbatical? Oh well, it can wait till my retirement. And I promise the University of Luton will not feature in the bit parodying a business school – City Business School watch out! One of the previous literary winners poses me the deeply philosophical question as to whether I believe it possible to survive such a function without being completely drunk. I answer in the affirmative. She disagrees. She espies an acquaintance: "Darling, that's the fourteenth time you've visited the toilet." Nobody on our table dares leave. Great joy at Joan Brady, age 54, winning the Whitbread Award for her novel Theory of War. *Part family history, the novel tells the story of Joan's grandfather, a white in slavery as an indentured labourer in the American South after the Civil War. Glad that a philistine at King Arthur's court who rarely finds time now to read a novel has been invited to such a prestige occasion.*

WEDNESDAY. *Meet with Marianne Lagrange of Paul Chapman, publishers, to discuss my edited text* Whistle Blowing in Society: Subversion or Corporate Citizenship? *Go through in detail. Discuss the need to avoid any libel in the text. Also the question of whether Robin Robison's chapter breaches the Official Secrets Act. Tell Marianne that the Cabinet Office and Treasury Solicitor have signed a release. They have demanded some small amendments which are all now in the public domain, and in any case of little consequence. This country is really obsessed with secrecy – it is the secrecy that permits some of those in power to hatch conspiracies against the general public they are supposed to be serving. It also allows them to wallow in their self-inspired view of their own importance. Sociology may be unpopular in some quarters, but Robert Michels certainly got it right in his "iron law of oligarchy" which observes the tendency in countries and organisations for small groups to divert the focus to their own interests, rather than that of other stakeholders.*

THURSDAY *Chair validation for University of Luton's* MSc *in waste management. A microcosm of the short-termism in higher education funding whereby the Higher Technology Training Council cuts off funding halfway through the postgraduate Dip, and left the university and students to do the shifty leg work to overcome the obstruction. Often wonder at validations whether some masters degrees will last for more than a year or two. Justifiable financially as a protracted short course, but difficult to justify as part of long-term strategic planning and commitment. Such is the brave new world of market focus and deregulation – the country full of half successful courses all indulging in splendid competition.*

Evening attend Freedom of Information Awards ceremony, with two awards being ones I had put forward: the John Lewis Partnership, with its encouragement in the in-house magazine of anonymous, critical debate, with answers provided for those needing them, and the "Swansea Four", three suspended and since reinstated, for blowing the whistle on poor academic standards.

FRIDAY. *Thank God It's Again (with apologies to Whitbread who owns the UK franchise).* ■

Chancellor's Address

Address by Sir David Plastow *on his Installation as*
Chancellor of the University of Luton

THANK YOU, VICE CHANCELLOR.

*May I begin by saying what a pleasure it was for me to be asked if I
would like to become the first Chancellor of the new University of
Luton. It was an invitation which I was delighted to accept, not least
because of my own personal association with the University, or rather
with one of its predecessors, Luton Technical College. I suppose all
graduates hope that in later life their Alma Mater will become a source
of support and inspiration. I could have asked for no greater honour
from mine, and I feel extremely privileged to have been given the
opportunity to become involved with the new university in this way. I
am deeply grateful to the University and the Board of Governors for the
trust that has been placed in me.*

*Not only is this an important day for me personally but it is also, of
course, a very important day for the University and for Luton itself. The
evolution of the former Luton Technical College into a fully fledged
university is something of which the town can be immensely proud.*

*But this kind of thing does not come about by accident. In this case it
is the result of a great deal of hard work, over a long period of time, by a
group of very able people, led by the Vice Chancellor himself. I would
like to take this opportunity to pay tribute, both to him and also to his
colleagues, for their ceaseless campaigning and dedication to a cause to
which they committed themselves totally, and which has resulted in the
beginning of an important new era for higher education in this town.*

*We should also pay tribute today to those great men and women of
earlier generations who were responsible for the development of the
original Technical Institute in Luton, and of its successors. We should not
forget that it was the educational facilities which they provided – not
only the Institute but also Luton College of Technology and Luton
College of Higher Education – which laid the foundations for the*

eventual establishment of the university itself.

Down the years their efforts helped to bring about a steady improvement in the educational facilities which the town could offer to young people from Luton itself as well as from elsewhere in the county. Today, of course, the march of progress means that students come here from all over the country and, indeed, from abroad.

For me, coming back to Luton for this ceremony today has been like coming home. I first moved to the town 43 years ago, when I began work as an engineering apprentice at Vauxhall. I lived here for eight years in all, and it was a very happy time for me. I became very fond of Luton – people here were always kind to this foreigner from far-off Lincolnshire, and made me feel genuinely welcome.

Soon after starting my apprenticeship at Vauxhall I began a day-release course at Luton Technical College, studying for an Ordinary National Certificate in mechanical engineering. I also became involved in the clubs and sporting activities which are such an important part of college life. From both the academic and social points of view, my time at the college is one on which I look back with great affection.

Some of my fondest memories of Luton are of Saturday afternoons spent watching the Hatters – that, by the way, for those of you who are not familiar with it, is the name by which Luton Town Football Club is known to its supporters. One of their stars – a great centre-half called Sid Owen – also played cricket, and many is the time that I had the honour of playing that other sport – the one involving willow and leather – with him, for Luton 2nd XI, at Wardown Park.

Wardown Park had other attractions for me as well in those days, as a certain young woman who worked in the museum next to the park meant rather a lot to me. I seem to remember spending an inordinate amount of time in that part of the town during those early years. It was surprising how even a young engineering apprentice who previously had never displayed any particular leaning towards archaeology or history could suddenly develop an obsessive interest in Stone Age flints and Anglo-Saxon coins.

Even St Mary's is familiar territory for me. Some years ago that same young woman from the museum was at my side in this very church, a few yards from where I am standing now, making her vow to love, cherish, honour and obey me. And I am very glad to say that she still does most of those things, although I have noticed that obeying seems to have gone out of fashion in recent years.

At the time of our wedding I was still an impecunious apprentice, and my newly acquired wife – who I am delighted to say is with me here today – was earning more money piecing together items of Roman pottery than I was piecing together motor cars on the assembly line at

Vauxhall. I suppose it means that for a time I was a kept man. It occurs to me that perhaps that is why she felt she didn't have to continue to obey me.

My eight years with Vauxhall, and the course I followed at Luton Technical College, set me on a path which led to a thoroughly rewarding career in industry, principally in the world of engineering and motor cars, of course, via Rolls-Royce to Vickers, and now to Inchcape. And I never forget that an integral part of my early progress at Vauxhall was the studying I undertook at the forerunner of this fine university.

In an increasingly competitive world, education has a vital role to play in helping the next generation to grasp whatever opportunities are presented to them in their careers. A growing number of the companies and organisations for which they will work when they move on from higher education will be international in their outlook, which means that in their business lives they are likely to be rubbing shoulders with highly qualified people from other countries too.

Standards of education throughout most of the developed world are improving steadily, and this university has an enormous responsibility in giving thousands of young people a sound academic basis on which to establish their careers. I am confident that it will meet this important challenge, and I pledge myself wholeheartedly to give whatever support I can in its endeavours.

I thank you for your welcome and greetings and I hope that we may serve together in pursuing the mission of our University with vigour and enthusiasm. ■

Epilogue

TONY WOOD

THE ATTAINMENT OF university status in the summer of 1993 caused a substantial, and unexpected, overshoot in full-time student numbers the following autumn. The subsequent accommodation pressures resulted in the university having to seek additional leasehold property for staff and students later in the year.

Immediate problems were also posed for the student accommodation service. At one stage 150 students were housed in local hotels at the university's expense while more permanent arrangements were made. Some adverse publicity ensued, which strengthened the resolve of governors to complete the current building programme whose objective was the completion of 1,500 units of purpose-built residential accommodation for the 1994 intake. This target was achieved.

During 1993–94 the government signalled its intention to introduce lengthy qualifying periods for future applicants for university status. With degree-awarding powers achieved, an applicant college would then have to demonstrate subsequent proficiency in applying those powers until further criteria had been met. The stiffest of these promised to be a target quota of students completing PhDs. It appeared inevitable that this would effectively close down further university designations for some time to come.

The government also announced a slowdown in the inexorable growth of higher education, effectively enforcing this by making swingeing reductions in fee levels, thereby making further expansion uneconomic. Those universities and colleges which had been slow to seize the earlier opportunities to expand were now unable to retrieve the situation, causing some financial and other problems. This policy did not cause difficulties at Luton, where the main period of expansion had already been completed.

Pressure continued to be exerted on students during 1993–94, through further reductions in the mandatory student grant. Increasing numbers across the country found themselves close to the poverty level, and the

141

situation in Luton was no exception. All universities found it necessary to create substantial hardship and related funds to help extreme cases. In the year following designation, the University of Luton distributed over £150,000 in vouchers and bursaries to 300 students, to assist with living, transport and child-care costs. It seemed likely the problem would worsen in the future rather than improve.

With the 1989 strategic plan (in its successively modified form) achieved, work immediately began on devising new medium- to long-term objectives. As student numbers had expanded during the early 1990s, class sizes had also increased substantially against a diminishing unit of resource (simply defined as the annual turnover divided by the number of full-time equivalent students). Because the growth had been so great at Luton, and its historical funding position as a college so low, the university possessed the lowest unit of funding per student in the sector. This required the institution to operate with super-efficiency, and while this attracted smiles of commendation from those in charge of the public purse, it placed very considerable pressures on all personnel. Major targets for the future therefore included rapid advances on the development of a student-centred curriculum and on opening up new revenue sources for the university. The completion of first-class facilities for student learning and staff research also rated as a high priority.

The emerging plan anticipated that the university would sustain its commitment to being primarily a teaching institution, with a strong underpinning of relevant research. Although the government of the day claimed to be seeking a stabilisation of the higher education sector to the turn of the century, few doubted that the pattern of adaptation and change established in recent years, in response to new political directions, would continue for many years to come.

Appendices

Appendix 1 Some significant events in the evolution of the University of Luton

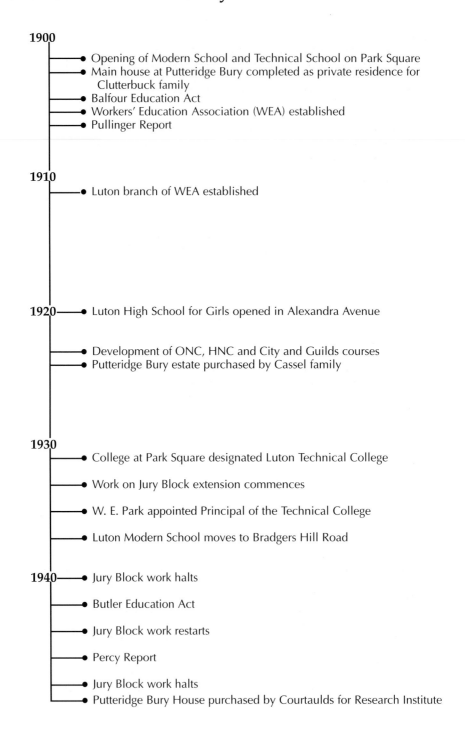

1900
- Opening of Modern School and Technical School on Park Square
- Main house at Putteridge Bury completed as private residence for Clutterbuck family
- Balfour Education Act
- Workers' Education Association (WEA) established
- Pullinger Report

1910
- Luton branch of WEA established

1920 — Luton High School for Girls opened in Alexandra Avenue
- Development of ONC, HNC and City and Guilds courses
- Putteridge Bury estate purchased by Cassel family

1930
- College at Park Square designated Luton Technical College
- Work on Jury Block extension commences
- W. E. Park appointed Principal of the Technical College
- Luton Modern School moves to Bradgers Hill Road

1940 — Jury Block work halts
- Butler Education Act
- Jury Block work restarts
- Percy Report
- Jury Block work halts
- Putteridge Bury House purchased by Courtaulds for Research Institute

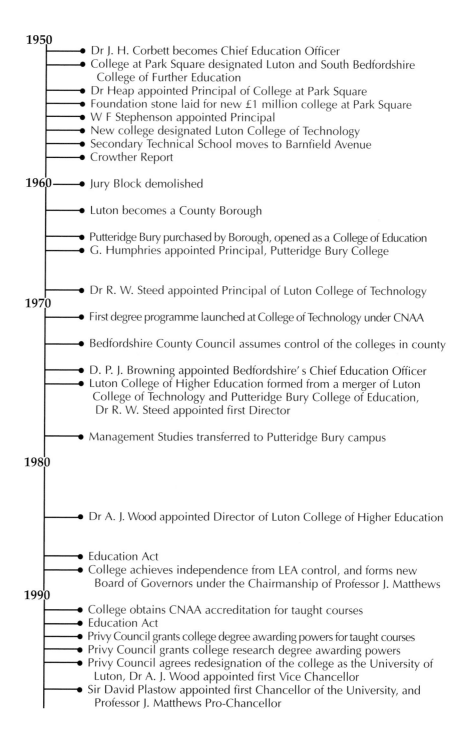

1950
- Dr J. H. Corbett becomes Chief Education Officer
- College at Park Square designated Luton and South Bedfordshire College of Further Education
- Dr Heap appointed Principal of College at Park Square
- Foundation stone laid for new £1 million college at Park Square
- W F Stephenson appointed Principal
- New college designated Luton College of Technology
- Secondary Technical School moves to Barnfield Avenue
- Crowther Report

1960
- Jury Block demolished

- Luton becomes a County Borough

- Putteridge Bury purchased by Borough, opened as a College of Education
- G. Humphries appointed Principal, Putteridge Bury College

- Dr R. W. Steed appointed Principal of Luton College of Technology

1970
- First degree programme launched at College of Technology under CNAA

- Bedfordshire County Council assumes control of the colleges in county

- D. P. J. Browning appointed Bedfordshire's Chief Education Officer
- Luton College of Higher Education formed from a merger of Luton College of Technology and Putteridge Bury College of Education, Dr R. W. Steed appointed first Director

- Management Studies transferred to Putteridge Bury campus

1980

- Dr A. J. Wood appointed Director of Luton College of Higher Education

- Education Act
- College achieves independence from LEA control, and forms new Board of Governors under the Chairmanship of Professor J. Matthews

1990
- College obtains CNAA accreditation for taught courses
- Education Act
- Privy Council grants college degree awarding powers for taught courses
- Privy Council grants college research degree awarding powers
- Privy Council agrees redesignation of the college as the University of Luton, Dr A. J. Wood appointed first Vice Chancellor
- Sir David Plastow appointed first Chancellor of the University, and Professor J. Matthews Pro-Chancellor

Appendix 2a Course validations, 1989–90

Course	Date	Type
Certificate in Education (CNAA) (joint with Hatfield Polytechnic)	13 Oct	Internal, resub
HND Estate Management (BTEC)	24 Oct	Internal, new
HNC/D Mechanical Engineering (BTEC) (joint with Bedford CHE)	3 Nov	Internal, resub
HNC/D Electronics (BTEC)	15 Nov	Internal, resub
HND Manufacturing Systems Eng (BTEC)	20 Nov	Internal, new
BA Community Management (CNAA)	20 Nov	Internal, new
HND Mech & Prod Eng (BTEC)	22 Nov	Internal, resub
HNC Building Studies (BTEC)	1 Dec	Internal, resub
Foundation Course in Accounting (Board of Accreditation)	15 Dec	Internal, resub
HNC Motor Vehicle Studies (BTEC)	9 Jan	Internal, resub
HNC Motor Vehicle Management (BTEC)	9 Jan	Internal, new
HNC Science (Chemistry) (BTEC)	18 Jan	Internal, resub
Advanced Diploma in English (LCHE)	9 Feb	Full, new
Postgraduate Diploma in Ecotoxicology (LCHE) (TA course)	19 Feb	Full, new
BSc Construction Management (CNAA)	15 Mar	Internal, new
BA Business Studies part-time (CNAA)	30 Mar	Internal, new
BSc Integrated Engineering with Management (CNAA)	3 Apr	Internal, new
Post Graduate Diploma in Marketing (CNAA)	24 Apr	Internal, new
BA Community Management (CNAA)	10 May	Joint
BA English and History (CNAA)	24 May	Internal, new
BSc Construction Management (CNAA)	25 May	Internal, new
BSc Integrated Engineering with Mgt (CNAA)	20 Jun	Joint
Postgraduate Diploma in Marketing (CNAA)	27 Jun	Joint
BA Bus. Studies full-time, Tourism Pathway (CNAA)	28 Jun	Full (delegated)
HNC Analytical Instrumentation (BTEC) (TA course)	2 Jul	Internal, new
Postgraduate Diploma in Software Eng Mgt (LCHE) (TA course)	2 Jul	Full, new
HNC Business Information Technology (BTEC) (TA course)	3 Jul	Internal, new
Diploma in Management Studies with IT (CNAA) (TA course)	3 Jul	Internal,new
BA Business Studies part-time (CNAA)	10 Jul	Joint

Notes: *Internal* refers to initial college event; *Full* refers to event with relevant validating body; *Joint* refers to an event with responsibility shared between college and a validating body; *Resub* refers to resubmission or revalidation of an existing course, though typically with major revisions

Appendix 2b Course validations, 1990–91

Event	Date	Course*
1	18 Sep	BSc (Hons) Construction Management
2	21 Sep	DMS with Information Technology
3	14 Nov	Access to Health and Social Studies
4	11 Dec	Foundation Course in Accounting
5	18 Feb	DMS (modular course)
6	25 Feb	NC/ND Motor Vehicle Engineering
7	5 Mar	BSc Construction Management
8	5 Mar	IIM Cert/Assoc Dip/PG Dip
9	7 Mar	Diploma HE in Midwifery
10	12 Mar	MA in Education Management
11	13 Mar	Diploma HE in Social Work and Diploma in Social Work
12	14 Mar	BSc (Hons) Combined Sciences - new pathways
13	18 Mar	BSc Building Surveying
14	20 Mar	LLB (Hons)
15	21 Mar	BA (Hons) Accounting and Finance
16	22 Mar	ACCA Level 2 full-time
17	12 Apr	PGDip/MSc Ecotoxicology and Pollution Monitoring
18	29 Apr	HNC/D Computer Studies
19	7 May	Diploma HE Midwifery
20	8 May	BSc (Hons) Combined Sciences - new pathways
21	9 May	LLB (Hons)
22	15 May	BA (Hons) Humanities
23	17 May	BSc (Hons) European Business Information Systems
24	21 May	Associateship of College of Preceptors
25	22 May	BA (Hons) Accounting and Finance
26	29 May	BSc Construction Management
27	4 Jun	BA (Hons) Media Studies
28	5 Jun	BSc (Hons) Combined Sciences - new pathways
29	6 Jun	BSc Building Surveying
30	18 Jun	PG Dip/MSc Ecotoxicology and Pollution Monitoring
31	1 Jul	BSc (Hons) Integrated Engineering with Management
32	3 Jul	LLB (Hons)
33	5 Jul	BSc Building Surveying
34	11 Jul	BSc (Hons) Information Systems for European Business
35	17 Jul	BA (Hons) Accounting
36	18 Jul	DMS (modular scheme)
37	24 Jul	BA (Hons) Media Studies
38	25 Jul	BSc (Hons) Environmental Management
39	13 Aug	Diploma HE Social Work and Diploma in Social Work

Note: *Where a course title is repeated it is because the course had to progress from internal to full validation

Appendix 2c Course validations, 1991–92

Course	Validating body	Internal validation	Final validation
General and cross-faculty courses			
College modular scheme	CNAA	25 Feb	7 Apr
BSc(Hons) Environmental Management (Pathway in college modular scheme)	CNAA	13 Jan	16 Apr
Faculty of Applied Sciences			
PG Dip in Software Engineering Mgt	CNAA	12 Mar	Apr/May
PG Dip in Analytical Instrumentation	LCHE	10 Mar	—
PG Dip in Computing with Humanities	CNAA	27 Feb	14 May
BSc (Hons) Business Information Systems	CNAA	30 Apr	17 Jun
HNC/D Computer Studies (review)	BTEC	(done)	4 Mar
HND Geographical Techniques (review)	BTEC	w/b 17 Feb	w/b 16 Mar
HND Geological Technology (review)	BTEC	30 Jan	w/b 16 Mar
BSc Combined Sciences – franchise to Dunstable College	CNAA	24 Mar	—
Faculty of the Built Environment			
HND Building Studies (Surveying)	BTEC	3 Mar	31 Mar
Faculty of Business			
PG Dip Business Decision Making	CNAA	3 Feb	14 Apr
BA (Hons) English	CNAA	17 Jan	25 Mar
Field within modular scheme:			
Marketing and Business	CNAA	11 Mar	12 Mar
Faculty of Engineering			
BSc Hons Integrated Eng with Mgt	CNAA	mid-Mar	11 May
HND Product Design (Dunstable College)	BTEC	26 Mar	May
Faculty of Health Care and Social Studies			
Fields in the modular scheme:			
Health Studies, Social Studies & Psychology	CNAA	11 Mar	13 May
ENB post-basic courses (902, 923, 936, 953, 997, 998)	ENB	5 Dec	—
ENB 870 Research Methodology	ENB	2 Mar	—
ENB 941, 978 (review)	ENB	21 May	—
BA (Hons) Public Administration and HNC/D Public Administration (review)	CNAA/BTEC	5 Mar	28 Apr
PG Dip Adult Guidance	CNAA	5 May	16 Jun
PG Dip Research Methods	CNAA	27 Apr	18 Jun
Occupational Health Nursing Diploma	CNAA/ENB	28 Feb	29 Apr
Faculty of Management			
Certificate in Education (Post Compulsory Ed)	CNAA	18 Oct	18/19 Mar
PG Dip/MSc Management of Technology	CNAA	26 Feb	15 Apr
MBA	CNAA	18 Mar	28 Apr
PG Dip Human Resource Management	CNAA	2 Apr	mid-May
PG Dip International Marketing	CNAA	13 May	late-Jun

Appendix 3 FT/SW subgraduate, undergraduate and postgraduate courses and fields 1992–93

Degree fields

Analytical Science
Biology
Biotechnology
Business
Community Management
Computer Science
English Studies
Environmental Management
Environmental Studies
Geology
Health Care
Health Studies

Information Systems
Integrated Engineering
Management Science
Mapping Science
Marketing
Modern Languages
Physical Geography
Psychology
Public Policy and Management
Quantitative Methods
Social Studies

Specialist degrees

Accounting
Building Surveying
Business Studies
Construction Management

Humanities
Law
Media Studies

Postgraduate courses

MSc Ecotoxicology and Pollution
  Monitoring
MSc Management of Technology
MBA
MA Guidance and Counselling
  of Adults
PG Dip Analytical Instrumentation

PG Dip Community Practice
PG Dip Computing with Humanities
PG Dip Employee Relations
PG Dip Human Resource Management
PG Dip Marketing
(Post Experience) Dip Management
  Studies

Diploma level courses

Dip HE Applied Social Studies
Dip HE Midwifery
Dip HE Nursing Studies
Dip HE Social Work
HND Building
HND Business and Finance
HND Business Information
  Technology
HND Computing
HND Electrical Engineering
HND Integrated Engineering
  (Mechatronics)

HND Land Administration
  (Estate Management)
HND Land Administration
  (Geographical Techniques)
HND Manufacturing Systems
  Engineering
HND Mechanical and Production
  Engineering
HND Public Administration
HND Science (Applied Biology)
HND Science (Geological Technology)

Appendix 4 FT/SW subgraduate, undergraduate and postgraduate courses and fields 1993–94

Degree fields in modular credit scheme

Access
Accounting
Animation
Architecture
Biology
Biotechnology
Business Administration
Business Decision Management
Business Studies
Business Systems
Building Surveying
Building Technology
Built Environment
Community Management
Comparative Literature
Computer Science
Contemporary History
Construction Management
Contemporary Writing in English
Digital Systems Design
Economics
Ecotoxicology and Pollution Studies
Educational Studies
English Studies
Environmental Analytical Chemistry
Environmental Management
Environmental Science
European Language Studies
European Regional Planning and
  Management
French
General Studies
Geography

Geology
German
Health Care
Health Science
Health Studies
Information Systems
Integrated Engineering
Italian
Journalism
Language and Area Studies
Law
Leisure Studies
Linguistics
Management Science
Mapping Science
Marketing
Media Production
Midwifery
Multimedia
Organisational Behaviour
Physical Geography
Professional Social Studies
Psychology
Public Policy and Management
Quantitative Methods
Regional Planning and Development
Social Studies
Spanish
Sports Science
Travel and Tourism
Video Production
Women's Health
Women's Studies

Postgraduate courses

MSc Business Decision Making
MSc Community Practice
MSc Ecotoxicology and Pollution
  Management
MSc Management of Technology
MBA
MA Guidance and Counselling for Adults
MA Human Resource Management
MA L2 Materials Development
MA Research and Evaluation for Practitioners
  in Health, Public and Social Services

PG Dip Analytical Instrumentation
PG Dip Community Practice
PG Dip Computing with Humanities
PG Dip Employee Relations
PG Dip Equal Opportunities
  Management
PG Dip Information Management
PG Dip Marketing
PG Dip Solid Waste Management
(Post-Experience) Diploma in
  Management Studies

Appendix 4 (continued)

Diploma level courses

Dip HE Applied Social Studies
Dip HE Nursing Studies
Dip HE Social Work
Diploma in Professional Studies (Acute Care)
Diploma in Professional Studies
  (Palliative Care)
HND Building
HND Business and Finance
HND Business Information Technology
HND Computing
HND Electrical Engineering
HND Environmental Analytical Chemistry

HND Environmental Science
HND Integrated Engineering
  (Mechatronics)
HND Land Administration
  (Estate Management)
HND Land Administration
  (Geographical Techniques)
HND Manufacturing Systems Engineering
HND Product Design
HND Public Administration
HND Science (Applied Biology)
HND Science (Geological Technology)

Appendix 5 Honorary awards to 1993

Honorary Fellowships

1989 Frank S. Lester, OBE, CEng, MRAeS, former Chairman of Governors
  and Mayor of Luton
  Professor J. M. Ashworth, DSc, FIBiol, Director, London School of
  Economics

1990 The Rt Reverend Chris J. Mayfield, Bishop of Wolverhampton
  Sam C. Whitbread

1991 Sir David Plastow, Chairman Inchcape plc
  Dr Roy W. Steed, BSc (Eng), PhD, CEng, MICE Mech, former Director,
  Luton College of Higher Education

1992 The Baroness Cox
  Alderman H C Lawrence, MBE, former Mayor of Luton

1993 Kelvin P. Hopkins, BA, former Chairman of Governors
  Graham Bright, MP, Luton South

Honorary Degrees (1993)

Honorary Doctor of Science
  Sir David Plastow, first Chancellor of the University
  Professor Malcolm Frazer, CBE, former Chief Executive, Council for
  National Academic Awards

Honorary Doctor of Arts
  Sir William Doughty, Chairman, North West Thames Regional Health
  Authority

Honorary Master of Business Administration
  John Barber, Director of Manufacturing, Vauxhall Motors Limited

Honorary Master of Technology
  John Shine, former Dean, Faculty of Construction, Luton College of
  Higher Education

Appendix 6 Members of the University Court

Sir David Plastow, Chancellor and Chairman of the Court

Professor J. Matthews, CBE, Pro-Chancellor, Chairman Board of Governors and Vice Chairman of the Court

Dr A. J. Wood, Vice Chancellor

Sir Neville Bowman-Shaw, former Chairman, Boss Trucks Ltd

Mr Graham Bright, MP, MP for Luton South

Sir Stuart Burgess, Chairman, Anglia & Oxford Regional Health Authority

Mr John Carlisle, MP, MP for Luton North

Mr Brian de la Salle, Supply Operations Director, Whitbread Beer Company and Chairman, Bedfordshire TEC

His Honour Judge Keith Devlin, Crown Court, Aylesbury

Mr Ian Dixon, Chairman, Willmott Dixon Ltd

Mr David Dunn, Chairman, Bletchley Motor Group plc

Mr Alan Dyer, Chief Constable of Bedfordshire

Mr Charles Golden, Chairman and Managing Director, Vauxhall Motors Ltd

Sir Nicholas Lyell, QC, MP, MP for Mid Bedfordshire and Attorney-General

Sir David Madel, MP, MP for South West Bedfordshire

Mr William Morris, General Secretary, Transport & General Workers' Union

Sir Stanley Odell, Chairman, South Bedfordshire Community Health Care NHS-Trust

Mrs Lucy Phillips, Luton Hoo

Sir Dai Rees, FRS, Secretary, Medical Research Council

Mr Adrian Shooter, Managing Director, Chiltern Train Operating Unit, British Railways Board

Mr Christopher Smallwood, Strategic Development Director and Group Economist, TSB Group plc

Mr Roger J Smith, Chairman, Central Holdings Ltd and Flitwick Holdings

Mr William Sowerby, Lilley Manor

Mr John Wotton, Managing Director, Huntleigh Technology plc

Appendix 7 Members of the Board of Governors (July 1993)

Independent Members (13, one vacancy – three-year term of office)

Professor J. Matthews, CBE (Chairman), former Director, AFRC Institute of Engineering Research

A. C. Lines (Vice Chairman), Personnel Manager, Vauxhall Motors Ltd

Ms J. Bonner, Director of Personnel, Monarch Airlines

S. Cuthbertson, Partner, Coopers & Lybrand Deloitte

Mrs A. Dongworth, Chief Executive, Luton & Dunstable NHS Trust

P. J. Henman, Chairman, T & E Neville Ltd

Mrs A. Higginson, Marketing & Training Director, Brook Street Bureau

P. Hoskins, Chief Executive, Luton, Bedford & District Chamber of Commerce

D. Ludlow, Chairman, Ludlow Group

D. A. Palmer, Financial consultant

G. Slessor, Assistant Divisional Organiser, Amalgamated Engineering Union

Dr A. L. Whitear, Director, Research & Development, Whitbread plc

Co-opted Members (seven, one vacancy – two-year term of office)

B. A. Howseman, Principal, Luton Sixth Form College

E. J. Stephens, Businessman and entrepreneur

J. R. C. Smith, nominated by the academic staff

Ms D. Bakewell, nominated by the non-teaching staff

County Councillor J. Thakoordin, Bedfordshire County Council

Rt Revd D. Farmbrough, Bishop of Bedford

Teaching Staff Nominee (one – two-year term of office)

S. Mortimer, nominated by the Academic Board

Student Nominee Member (one - one-year term of office)

J. Moore, ex officio, President, Student Union

The Vice Chancellor of the University (one)

Dr A. J. Wood, Vice Chancellor

Appendix 8 Members of staff at the time of designation as the University of Luton, July 1993

Mrs W. M. Abbott **N**
Miss S. Abdullah **SS**
Mrs B. Acharya **L**
Mr D. Acharya **L**
Dr R. Adams **PB**
Mr O. N. Adjei **AS**
Mr D. Affleck-Green **H**
Miss V. J. Ahearne **E**
Mrs S. Ahmed **E**
Dr K. Ahmet **DT**
Mr W. Aitken **DT**
Mr S. R. Akhurst **DT**
Mr H. O. Akin-Rinade **EB**
Mrs S. V. Aldcroft **HC**
Mr P. R. Alford **B**
Mrs M. Alfred **F**
Miss J. I. Ali **MS**
Miss N. Ali **HC**
Miss S. Ali-Khan **B**
Mr R. T. Allen **DT**
Mrs W. F. Allen **F**
Mr D. R. Allum **AS**
Mr A. Ambridge **H**
Mr C. R. Anderson **H**
Mr D. G. Anderson **AS**
Miss P. W. Anderson **PB**
Mr M. P. Anderton **SS**
Mr H. R. Andrew **AS**
Mrs V. E. Angliss **HC**
Mr M. J. Anstey **CEA**
Mrs P. Archell **C**
Mr N. J. Arthur **B**
Mrs P. Arthur **B**
Mrs H. Ashby **COM**
Mr J. V. Ashby **PB**
Mrs J. E. Aspin **HC**
Mrs E. Atchison **HC**
Dr A. Atkinson **AR**
Dr A. L. Atkinson **CEA**
Mr S. R. Atkinson **AS**
Mr S. Aubeeluck **HC**
Mrs S. V. Ayling **SS**
Mrs K. Ayres **PB**

Miss S. Bachini **MS**
Mr S. Badman **L**
Mr J. M. Bailey **E**

Mr R. B. Bailey **B**
Mr D. J. Baker **F**
Mrs J. Baker **B**
Mr M. F. Baker **DT**
Miss D. Bakewell **AS**
Mr G. J. Balfour-Layden **DT**
Mr M. R. Ball **DT**
Dr B. Baluch **HC**
Mr J. Banham **CS**
Mrs A. Banks-Smith **SC**
Mr M. E. Banyard **AS**
Ms S. Baptiste **CS**
Miss K. Barden **B**
Mr D. Barnsley **B**
Mr R. Barrett **L**
Mr C. Barton **MS**
Ms M. J. Barton **COM**
Ms S. Basra **HC**
Mrs D. M. Bastiani **CS**
Mr N. L. Bateson **B**
Dr M. G. Batham **AS**
Miss D. A. Beadle **B**
Mrs P. Beagle **HC**
Mr R. Beard **AS**
Miss R. F. Beaumont **HC**
Mr J. R. Beaumont-Kerridge **B**
Mrs W. G. Beckett **HC**
Miss A. C. Bedeau **HC**
Mrs D. Bedward **M**
Mrs F. Bee **B**
Mr D. W. Beetham **DT**
Ms B. V. Bell **M**
Mr M. Benner **L**
Mr J. B. Bennett **B**
Dr D. Berridge **HC**
Mrs R. D. Betts **HC**
Mr I. Beveridge **EO**
Mr S. A. Beynon **DT**
Mr R. C. Bhanot **EO**
Mrs H. E. B. Bharmal **DT**
Mr N. A. Bharmal **HC**
Mrs A. Bianco **F**
Mrs G. Bianco **F**
Mr A. E. Bibb **FI**
Mr I. R. Billington **HC**
Prof. P. Birch **AS**
Dr D. J. Bird **AS**

Mr L. Blackband **AS**
Mr C. Blackburn **AS**
Mrs D. L. Blackmore **B**
Mr J. F. Blake **AS**
Mrs M. Bloxham **SS**
Ms G. Boachie-Freeman **FI**
Mr T. Boatswain **H**
Mrs Y. L. Bolin **HC**
Mrs J. E. Bond **C**
Miss J. L. Bone **AS**
Mr H. K. Bose **DT**
Mrs L. B. Boston **CS**
Mrs R. J. Bottoms **HC**
Mrs M. S. Bozier **DT**
Mr M. Braithwaite **B**
Mr J. A. Brammer **DT**
Mr J. H. Bramwell **AS**
Mr J. Brannigan **H**
Mrs C. A. Brennan **C**
Mr A. Brett **DT**
Mrs E. A. Briars **PB**
Mr R. Briars **PB**
Mr I. R. Bridgeman **H**
Ms P. E. G. Bridger **C**
Mr P. W. Brooks **DT**
Mrs C. E. A. Brooka **CEA**
Mr C. Brown **PB**
Mr D. G. L. Brown **DT**
Mrs G. M. Brown **HC**
Mr R. W. Brown **CEA**
Mrs T. Brown **F**
Mr A. Bull **DT**
Mr A. Bullimore **L**
Mr F. C. Bullock **FI**

Miss V. Bullon **B**
Dr S. T. Bunker **H**
Mrs B. J. Burden **HC**
Mrs D. Burgess **MAR**
Mr G. H. Burgess **DT**
Miss V. M. Burke **B**
Ms D. J. Burkhardt **AS**
Mrs A. Burnage **MC**
Ms C. Burnley **H**
Mrs A. L. Burton **D**
Mrs G. R. Burton **PB**
Mrs K. Burton **AS**
Mrs A. E. Bushnell **AS**
Miss R. Butler **CEA**
Mr R. Bywaters **DT**

Mr D. E. Cachin **PB**
Mr M. Cahill **DT**
Mrs C. Calbeck **PB**
Mr J. A. Callaghan **EB**
Mrs J. M. Callaghan **F**
Mr P. M. Callaghan **F**
Mr B. Callard **M**
Mr S. Camiah **HC**
Miss C. M. Canning **HC**
Mrs S. T. Cannon **F**
Miss M. B. Canny **B**
Mr J. Caplan **DT**
Mr A. Capp **DT**
Ms C. Carby **EO**
Mr R. P. Carman **B**
Dr F. W. Carr **M**
Mrs J. M. Carr **CS**
Mrs Y. J. Carroll **DT**

AR Applied Research
AS Applied Sciences
B Business
C Catering
CEA Centre for External Affairs
COM Communication Services
CS Computer Services
D Directorate
DT Design & Technology
E Enterprise
EB Estates & Buildings
EO Educational Opportunities
F Facilities
FI Finance

H Humanities
HC Health Care & Social Studies
L Library
LR Learning Resources
M Management
MAR Marketing
MS Management Services
N Nursery
P Personnel
PAY Payroll
PB Putteridge Bury
QA Quality Assurance
R Registry SC Short Courses
SS Student Services

Appendix 8 (continued)

Mr G. S. Carter **MS**

Mrs L. J. Cassidy **C**

Ms D. Cato **F**

Ms C. Chadney **EO**

Mr P. B. Chambers **SS**

Mrs S. Chandler **PB**

Mrs J. C. Chapman **PB**

Miss M. Chapman **PB**

Mrs O. Charters **HC**

Mrs J. Chin **L**

Mr A. Chmielewski **H**

Mrs J. B. Christopher **L**

Mr J. C. T. Chuah **B**

Mrs P. J. N. Church **PB**

Mr E. J. Churcher **M**

Miss R. M. Cives-Enriques **H**

Dr M. J. Clapson **H**

Mrs D. Claridge **L**

Mr A. G. Clark **AS**

Mr D. J. Clark **CS**

Miss H. S. Clark **MS**

Mr R. N. Clark **DT**

Mr S. A. Clarke **B**

Mr R. Clarke **DT**

Mrs M.P. Clayton **PB**

Mrs J. Clements **PB**

Mrs J. Cline **FI**

Mr D. G. Cloonan **F**

Mrs E. W. Coakes **B**

Dr P. C. Coggins **AS**

Mr T. Cole **B**

Ms A. P. Coleman **F**

Ms J. Coleman **M**

Mrs S. Collington **F**

Mr A. Collins **LR**

Mrs E. R. Collins **B**

Mr R. K. Common **HC**

Mr T. J. J. Connor **M**

Mr K. A. F. Cook **D**

MRS V. M. Cooke **HC**

Mrs M. I. Cooper **F**

Mr A. D. Cooper **AS**

Mr M. P. Cooper **HC**

Ms M. Cordt **F**

Miss M. Cosby **F**

Mr J. P. Coulter **AS**

Mrs M. Covington **HC**

Mr J. Cowan **B**

Mr D. Cowell **MS**

Mrs S. Cowell **MS**

Mr S. B. Cowell **MS**

Dr J. M. Cowley **H**

Miss J. M. Cox **HC**

Mr M. D. Cracknell **HC**

Mr T. J. Cranvey **MS**

Ms S. Crawshaw **COM**

Miss S. Crocker **MS**

Mrs R. Compton **B**

Miss A. H. Cronin **HC**

Mr D. Cronin **F**

Mrs S. K. Crook **HC**

Mr R. Cross **PB**

Mr K. R. Crossley **AS**

Mr S. E. Croucher **DT**

Mr M. G. Cruttenden **EB**

Dr B. P. Crystal **E**

Mr R. C. Cullen **EB**

Mrs M. Cummins **C**

Mrs E. Cunningham **F**

Mr J. Cunningham **CS**

Miss J. M. Cupid **F**

Mrs M. R. Currie **HC**

Mrs M. J. D'Angelis **F**

Mrs A. Da-Roza **HC**

Mrs H. T. Dagley **PB**

Mrs W. P. Dagley **PB**

Mr M. Dalal **CEA**

Ms D. P. Dalton **PB**

Mr K. Daniels **L**

Mr P. D. Darling **H**

Mr M. B. Dauharry **HC**

Mr I. David **B**

Mrs F. B. Davies **AS**

Mr P.A. Davies **B**

Ms H. Davis **HC**

Mrs J. Davis **MS**

Ms S. A. Davis **HC**

Miss C. L. V. Davison **DT**

Mrs S. A. Dawes **CS**

Mr C. F. De Vita **B**

Mrs A. J. Deacon **L**

Mrs E. M. Deacon **PB**

Miss S. Deacon **HC**

Dr H. Dean **HC**

Mr P. J. Dean **H**

Mr R. E. Dean **DT**

Mrs M. C. Decent **HC**

Mrs L. J. Deed **N**
Mr J. A. Dennis **HC**
Mr D. J. Dent **DT**
Mr J. S. Derfurt **CS**
Mrs M. Devane **C**
Mr D. Dewson **EB**
Mr W. M. Diack **MS**
Miss S. Y. Dias **CS**
Mr C. Dibben **AS**
Mr J. H. Dickens **HC**
Ms J. Dickson **HC**
Mr M. Dillon **HC**
Mr C. K. R. Dixon **B**
Mrs P. Dixon **HC**
Dr P. G. Dixon **HC**
Mrs J. Dobberson **N**
Mr A. P. H. Dobson **DT**
Ms J. E. Dodd **QA**
Miss S. L. Dodd **PB**
Ms S. Doherty **FI**
Mr J. S. Dolan **AS**
Mrs F. Donaldson **F**
Mr A. P. Dorothy **DT**
Mrs S. Douglas **COM**
Mr M. J. Downing **DT**
Dr M. J. Downward **AS**
Miss P. Doyle **AS**
Mrs J. M. Drage **L**
Mr R. M. Driver **R**
Ms Y. M. Du Casse **HC**
Miss H. R. Duckett **R**
Mr R. D. Dudley **COM**
Miss A. Duensing **H**
Mrs K. M. Duggan **MS**

Dr A. M. Duncan **AS**
Dr M. Dunckley **AS**
Miss J. Dunn **F**
Mr K. P. Dunn **PB**
Mr M. B. Dunne **L**

Dr C. Eccles **AS**
Mrs D. Edler **R**
Mrs D. M. Edmonds **N**
Mr C. G. Edwards **B**
Mrs M. Edwards **M**
Mr M. K. Edwards **FI**
Mr R. A. Edwards **PB**
Mr C. A. Elliott **DT**
Mr T. N. Elliott **F**
Mr G. Ellis **B**
Mr I. Ellis **CEA**
Ms K. Ellis **HC**
Dr P. V. Ellis **HC**
Mr R. J. S Ellis **CS**
Miss S. J. Ellis **DT**
Mrs S. Elwes **B**
Mrs M. A. Engstrom **C**
Mrs P. V. Engstrom **C**
Mr C. D. Evans **DT**
Mr C. N. Evans **DT**
Dr G. H. Evans **AS**
Mrs R. Evans **EO**
Mr R. P. Ewer **DT**

Ms F. Fahr **AS**
Dr A. R. Fallone **HC**
Dr S. J. Fallows **EO**
Mrs J. D. Fanghanel **H**

AR Applied Research
AS Applied Sciences
B Business
C Catering
CEA Centre for External Affairs
COM Communication Services
CS Computer Services
D Directorate
DT Design & Technology
E Enterprise
EB Estates & Buildings
EO Educational Opportunities
F Facilities
FI Finance

H Humanities
HC Health Care & Social Studies
L Library
LR Learning Resources
M Management
MAR Marketing
MS Management Services
N Nursery
P Personnel
PAY Payroll
PB Putteridge Bury
QA Quality Assurance
R Registry SC Short Courses
SS Student Services

Appendix 8 (continued)

Mr G. Farmer **AS**
Miss N. Farooq **P**
Mrs B. E. Fearn **F**
Mrs S. Fearnley **R**
Mrs S. Fensom **HC**
Mrs A. Fensome **F**
Dr A. A. Finch **AS**
Ms S. Finch **E**
Mrs J. Findley **L**
Dr J. M. K. Fitch **HC**
Mrs R. F. Fitches **HC**
Mrs L. Fitzgerald **HC**
Mr M. J. Fletcher **DT**
Dr A. J. Forrester **AS**
Mr G. Fortune **DT**
Mr D. Foster **AS**
Mr M. J. Foster **DT**
Mrs W. M. Foster **HC**
Mrs P. Foulkes **M**
Mrs E. Fountain **MS**
Mrs O. M. Fowler **SS**
Mr M.R. Fox **DT**
Mrs M. Frampton **N**
Mrs B. Francisque **F**
Mr J. Franklin **DT**
Mr K. J. Fraser **HC**
Mrs J. Frederick **F**
Ms S. L. Freedman **L**
Mr S. French **CS**
Mr T. S. French **AS**
Mrs V. French **HC**
Mr I. W. Fribbance **HC**
Mr M. Fulton **E**

Miss T. K. Gaffney **FI**
Mrs P. T. J. Gallagher **C**
Mrs R. Gallagher **F**
Miss L. M. Gallimore **PB**
Mr M. J. Gamble **COM**
Mrs A. F. Garner **AS**
Miss G. E. Garrett **SC**
Mrs P. Gbogboade **F**
Mr A. Geeson **L**
Mrs C. B. Gibbins **MS**
Mr D. R. Gibson **DT**
Mrs J. Gicquel **PB**
Mr M. R. Gillard **SS**
Mrs S. E. Gillard **AS**
Mr F. J. Gingell **DT**

Mrs L. M. Gittins **R**
Miss T. Gladding **AS**
Mrs S. E. Glenister **SS**
Mr W. J. Glew **DT**
Miss E. Gonzalez **H**
Miss C. A. Gordon **MS**
Mrs C. A. Gower **PB**
Mr C. P. Grabowski **B**
Mr M. N. Graham **F**
Miss J. Grail **DT**
Mr J. Grainger **P**
Mr C. T. Grant **EB**
Mr M. R. Grant **AS**
Ms G. Gray **C**
Mrs J. Gray **MS**
Dr J. S. Gray **AS**
Mr P. D. Gray **HC**
Miss P. Grayson **P**
Mrs I. Green **PB**
Mr P. D. Green **MC**
Mrs C. Greenidge **F**
Mr R. K. Greenidge **F**
Ms I. Greenwood **B**
Mr W. R. Greig **B**
Mrs B. E. Grieve **L**
Mr S. W. Grifin **H**
Mrs S. N. Griffiths **HC**
Mrs I. Groom **C**
Miss J. C. M. Guegan **H**
Mr K. R. Guest **EO**
Mr A. Gulliver **M**
Mrs J. E. Gurth **H**

Mr R. A. Hadland **B**
Mr D. Haestier **DT**
Mrs S. Haestier **PB**
Dr B. G. D. Haggett **CEA**
Mrs H. W. Hale **PB**
Miss B. D. Halford **HC**
Mr M. J. Halfpenny **F**
Mr D. Hall **M**
Mrs J. A. Hall **MS**
Mr R. V. Hall **DT**
Miss E. J. Hallam **HC**
Mr A. S. Halstead **H**
Mrs I. S. Halstead **H**
Mr B. Hamblin **DT**
Prof D. J. Hamblin **PB**
Mr Y. Hamed **AS**

Mr J. C. Hamer **B**
Mrs M. M. Hamilton **FI**
Mrs C. M. Hanks **HC**
Ms C. J. Hannah **HC**
Mr I. Hardaker-Jones **F**
Mr L. A. Harding **SS**
Mrs S. E. Hardy **HC**
Mr A. J. Hare **CS**
Dr R. D. Harper **AS**
Mr R. W. Harris **QA**
Mr R. C. Harvey **DT**
Mr N. Hashmi **CS**
Mr J. A. Hassall **DT**
Mrs C. Havill **HC**
Mrs J. E. Hawkins **HC**
Mr R. Hawkins **MS**
Mrs R. E. D. Hawkins **B**
Miss A. Hayes **L**
Mr P. Haysom **CS**
Mrs K. Hayton **H**
Mr N. Hayward **CS**
Miss J. M. Hazell **DT**
Miss J. Hazle **MS**
Dr R. Hearing **DT**
Mr R. E. Hearn **COM**
Dr D. J. Heath **AS**
Dr B. Heins **H**
Mrs T. I. V. Heley **MS**
Mr R. Hempenstall **EB**
Mrs B. D. Henderson **HC**
Miss J. P. Hendrickson **SS**
Ms P. A. Herber **HC**
Mr I. F. Hesketh **AS**
Miss C. Hewer **E**

Mrs E. S. Hide **HC**
Mr R. S. Hill **DT**
Mr M. A. Hilton **HC**
Mrs S. K. Hindler **AS**
Miss C. Hindley **PB**
Mrs H. Hinds **L**
Mr L. J. Hockley **H**
Mrs J. A. Holding **B**
Mrs V. J. Holland **PB**
Mr J. P. Holmes **EB**
Mrs J. Holroyd **B**
Mrs J. I. Holt **C**
Mr M. Hook **CS**
Ms S. A. Horsey **B**
Mr B. Hough **P**
Mr E. Hounslow **H**
Mrs C. F. Howarth **PB**
Mrs E. A. Howarth **C**
Mr M. G. Hudson **AS**
Mr I. R. Hughes **DT**
Mrs P. E. Hughes **HC**
Mr T. C.Hughes **COM**
Mrs G. Hunkin **HC**
Mr B. Hunt AS
Mrs B. Hunt **C**
Ms A. K. Huszcza **HC**
Ms C. Hutchinson **N**
Mr J. Hutchinson **H**
Mr C. J. Hyde **COM**
Mr P. J. Hyde **DT**
Mrs J. A. Hyland **HC**

Mrs L. Iacono **F**
Miss A. Iannaccone **H**

Appendix 8 (continued)

Miss M. Iannibelli **AS**
Ms P. C. Igbolekwu **HC**
Mrs M. Ingham **HC**
Mrs A. Ingram-Forde **H**
Mr M. Iqbal **AS**
Mrs L. M. Irvine **C**

Miss L. Jackson **B**
Mrs F. Jacobs **MS**
Mr A. Jamal **CS**
Mrs J. C. Jarvis **MS**
Mr J. L. Jeffries **B**
Mr G. L. Jeffs **DT**
Mrs A. M. Jennings **C**
Mr R. J. Jeyes **FI**
Dr D. T. John **D**
Mr C. C. Johns **HC**
Mrs M. Johnson **C**
Dr M. G. Johnson **H**
Miss S. Johnson **F**
Mrs S. J. Johnson **L**
Mr N. Johnston **AS**
Miss A. Jones **B**
Mrs M. Jones **PB**
Dr M. C. Jones **M**
Mr D. Joseph **CS**
Mr T. A. Joyce **DT**
Mr D. Jugessur **HC**
Mrs M. C. A. Julien **FI**

Ms J. Kavanagh **SS**
Miss A. Kay **SS**
Miss E. C. Kay **COM**
Mr S. M. Kayani **CS**
Mr P. J. Keay **AS**
Mrs M. J. Keegan **F**
Mr R. W. Keen **CS**
Mr M. Kelly **B**
Miss M. M. Kelly **M**
Mr P. Kelly **AS**
Mr T. W. J. Kelly **F**
Mr S. D. Kendall **MS**
Ms A. L. Kennedy **EO**
Mr T. Khan **B**
Dr U. A. Khan **HC**
Mr Z. G. Khan **HC**
Mr S. Khanchandani **CED**
Mr A. King **H**
Mrs D. E. King **M**

Mr P. R. Kingsbury **PB**
Mr R. S. Kinman **B**
Mrs M. Kirby **SC**
Mrs J. M. Knight **B**
Ms J. M. Knight **H**
Mrs C. Knights **P**
Ms J. Knowl es **EO**
Mrs S. R. L. Kowalczuk **L**

Mrs L. La-Vita **F**
Ms B. J. Lacey **SS**
Mrs C. E. Ladley **L**
Dr P. D. Ladley **AS**
Ms J. Lafferty **B**
Mrs J. Laird **AS**
Mrs G. M. Lake **P**
Miss V. J. Lake **P**
Mrs P. A. Lancaster **HC**
Mr D. V. Lansfield **CS**
Mrs B. A. Large **SS**
Dr A. C. Larrea **H**
Mr C. J. Lathwell **DT**
Mr S. Latimer **B**
Mr D. W. Lauder **B**
Dr L. A. Lawrence **B**
Miss J. A. Leadbetter **COM**
Miss L. S. Leader **N**
Mr J. R. Lee **HC**
Ms L. F. E. Lee **B**
Mrs C. J. Leech **D**
Mr R. G. Leech **DT**
Mr B. A. Lehaney **B**
Mr A. A. Lettman **PB**
Mr P. B. J. Lewarne **DT**
Mrs K. L. Lewis **PB**
Mr M. Lewis **DT**
Ms M. E. Lewis **SS**
Mr R. Lewis **B**
Mrs C. Lewis-Villien **H**
Mr K. Lim **HC**
Mrs J. M. Lindsay **C**
Mrs L. A. Lindsley **PB**
Mr D. G. Lingwood **B**
Mr T. S. Linney **DT**
Mr A. D. Lisle **DT**
Mr J. Lisle **B**
Mr B. T. Lloyd **AS**
Mr A. J Lloyd-Payne **DT**
Mr R. Lockie **HC**

Mr L. Lockton **L**
Mr J. W. E. Lodge **B**
Miss H. J. Lomax **HC**
Mrs M. Lombardi **F**
Miss P. Loughlin **MS**
Mr J. G. Loughran **DT**
Ms K. Love **M**
Mr A. Loynes **PB**
Ms V. F. Lucus **HC**
Mrs A. Lukes **AS**
Mr N. Lusby **DT**

Ms A. Maclaren **M**
Ms A. Maclean **B**
Mrs A. Macready **SS**
Ms T. M. Makin **AS**
Mr M. D. Malactos **AS**
Mr N. J. Malone **H**
Miss M. G. Manca **AS**
Mrs J. M. Manley **D**
Mrs J. R. Mann **M**
Mr S. Mann **F**
Mrs P. Mann **P**
Ms A. M. Mannell **FI**
Mr R. Manser **M**
Mr A. R. Manser **F**
Dr A. Mansour **AS**
Ms K. March **EO**
Mrs J. K. Mardle **HC**
Mr S. B. Mardlin **P**
Mr R. A. Marlow **F**
Mrs M. A. Marshall **PB**
Mr A. Martin **EB**
Mrs D. H. Martin **F**

Mr E. Martin **DT**
Mr J. H. Martin **DT**
Mr L. B. R. Martin **DT**
Miss L. M. Martin **CS**
Miss S. P. Martin **AS**
Mr I. A. Mason **AS**
Ms G. Mathieson **MAR**
Mr S. C. Mathieson **MAR**
Mr I. Mathurin **DT**
Mrs C. A. Matthews **M**
Mr D. E. Matthews **AS**
Mrs H. Maxted **CEA**
Mr T. May **B**
Miss S. A. Mayne **B**
Miss F. M. McCabe **EO**
Ms V. McCabe **AS**
Mrs N. A. McCarthy **CS**
Mrs B. McClure **M**
Mrs E. B. McConkey **H**
Mr W. J. McConnell **AS**
Mr D. J. McCool **DT**
Mr D. M. McDermott **SS**
Miss M. McDonnell **H**
Mrs K. P. McElroy **C**
Mr D. H. McErlean **H**
Mrs V. A. McEvoy **HC**
Mr R. McEwan **PB**
Miss D. McGerty **L**
Miss G. M. McGibbon **SS**
Miss J. McGovern **F I**
Miss R. A. McGuire **CS**
Mrs J. McInnis **F**
Ms A. McKenna **L**
Mr A. M. McKenzie **SS**

AR Applied Research
AS Applied Sciences
B Business
C Catering
CEA Centre for External Affairs
COM Communication Services
CS Computer Services
D Directorate
DT Design & Technology
E Enterprise
EB Estates & Buildings
EO Educational Opportunities
F Facilities
FI Finance

H Humanities
HC Health Care & Social Studies
L Library
LR Learning Resources
M Management
MAR Marketing
MS Management Services
N Nursery
P Personnel
PAY Payroll
PB Putteridge Bury
QA Quality Assurance
R Registry **SC** Short Courses
SS Student Services

161

Appendix 8 (continued)

Mr T. P. McKeown **F**
Mr P. McKinley **F**
Mr M. J. McKnight **MS**
Mr D. McLean **DT**
Mrs I. T. McLeod **B**
Mr S. McLeod **DT**
Mrs B. McNamee **C**
Mr C. P. Meadows **DT**
Dr R. Melrose **H**
Mrs S. A. Melville **HC**
Mrs K. K. Merchant **B**
Mrs B. Messina **F**
Mr F. Michaelson **AS**
Mrs M. Miles **R**
Mr M. J. Miles **DT**
Ms M. M. Miles **H**
Mr A. Millar **DT**
Mr A. Millard **AS**
Miss A. Millen **H**
Mr D. Miller **PB**
Mr F. J. Milligan **HC**
Mr B. Mills **DT**
Mrs J. Miners **E**
Mrs M. G. Minter **MS**
Mr H. Mirza **CS**
Dr R. Misra **AS**
Mr D. Mitchell **DT**
Mr H. Mitchell **SS**
Mr I. J. Mitchell **PB**
Mr M. R. Mitchell **HC**
Mr P. N. Mitchell **CS**
Dr W. A. Mitchell **AS**
Mrs S. Modi **AS**
Mrs G. Moloney **PB**
Mrs J. M. Monaco **AS**
Mr J. Monahan **DT**
Mr A. J. Monk **DT**
Prof J. W. Montgomery **B**
Mrs V. G. Montgomery **L**
Mrs F. Monzione **F**
Mr D. J. Moon **DT**
Mr A. Moore **M**
Ms W. Moore **SS**
Mr I. Moran **SS**
Mr C. R. Morey **AS**
Mrs J. Morgan **C**
Ms V, Morris **B**
Miss M. L. Morrison **FI**
Mr S. Mortimer **DT**

Mr P. J. Moulsley **DT**
Mr W. R. Mulcaster **B**
Miss D. M. Muldoon **B**
Mr A. Munt **DT**
Dr A. J. Murkett **AS**
Mr N. M. Murphy **DT**
Mr S. Mylott **CS**
Mr B. F. Mynard **EB**

Mrs K. Nairn **F**
Mr L. Nanton **F**
Mrs H. Naranbhai **HC**
Mrs J. P. Nasseri **F**
Mrs C. G. Naughton **B**
Mrs P. Nelms **HC**
Mr W. Nelson **CEA**
Mr P. E.J. Neville **H**
Mr C. H. Newby **CS**
Mrs J. A. Newman **F**
Mrs V. A. Newman **CEA**
Mr J. C. Nichol **AS**
Mr M. J. Nicholson **DT**
Mr I. Nicol **FI**
Miss C. Norris **CEA**
Mr G. Notcutt **AS**
Mr W. D. Ntale **EB**

Mrs C. O'Brien **MS**
Miss J. A. O'Connor **SS**
Mrs J. O'Dell **COM**
Mr A. O'Dowd **SS**
Mr E. J. O'Neill **B**
Ms M. O'Neill **PB**
Mr M. A. O'Regan **HC**
Dr M. T. O'Rourke **H**
Mr C. Oakley **PB**
Mr D. J. Oakeley **DT**
Mrs S. M. Oakley **PB**
Mr M. A. Olaseinde **B**
Miss D. Y. Oliver **HC**
Mr S. A. Orchard **AS**
Mr D. A. Orwin **AS**
Mr C. P. Osborn **DT**
Mr A. G. Osborne **M**
Ms M. Owens **HC**

Dr A. Page **H**
Mr A. H. Page **H**
Mr B. C. Pain **B**

Mrs Y. Pain **L**
Mrs R. Panchal **AS**
Miss T. Papaloizou **AS**
Mrs Z. A. Parkar **MS**
Mrs J. Parrett **CS**
Mrs J. Parry **HC**
Mrs J. E. Parsons **AS**
Mr M. J. Parsons **PB**
Ms S. K. Parsons **COM**
Mr D.R. Patel **CS**
Mr M. R. Patel **DT**
Mr N. V. Patel **B**
Miss S. Patel **MS**
Mr P. Patrick **PB**
Dr J. Pattison **AS**
Mrs B. Paull **HC**
Mr C. Pearson **HC**
Mrs A. J. Peck **B**
Mrs B. A. Peck **MS**
Mr R. F. Peck **M**
Miss S. Peel **MS**
Mr A. Peerbhoy **AS**
Mr H. Peffers **EB**
Mr P. Perels **DT**
Mr J. Perrin **DT**
Mr M. J. Perry **F**
Mr G. Pethybridge **EB**
Miss M. R. Petit-Rafer **B**
Mr P. A. Phillips **AS**
Miss J. K. Pickard **FI**
Mrs R. Pinto **QA**
Mrs J. R. Pitcher **AS**
Mrs A. J. Pitchford **M**
Mr S. Plant **PB**

Mr J. C. Plater **AS**
Miss A. S. Platt **B**
Mr C. J. Plummer **PB**
Mr D. Plummer **COM**
Mrs S. Porter **C**
Mr G. Powell **AS**
Miss A. Power **AS**
Mr S. R. Powers **H**
Mrs S. Pratt **F**
Ms S. J. Primmer **MAR**
Ms M. Prince **F**
Mr s K. N. Pritchett **HC**
Mrs G. Procaccini **F**
Mrs M. G. A. Puch **M**
Dr N. R. Punchard **AS**
Mrs A. L. Punter **PB**
Mrs S. Purdy **AS**
Mr A. E. Pyne **PB**

Mr M. J. Raine **DT**
Ms J. Ramsay **HC**
Mr I. M. Ramshaw **CS**
Mrs R. Ramshaw **L**
Mr G. S. Randhawa **HC**
Mr J. T. Rankin **COM**
Prof D. M. Rawson **CEA**
Mr M. J. Rawson **M**
Miss H. L. Read **HC**
Ms C. Rees **SS**
Ms C. R. Rees **AS**
Mrs L. S. Relph **DT**
Miss K. Rew **DT**
Ms C. M. Rexworthy **PB**
Miss J. C. Reynolds **CS**

AR Applied Research
AS Applied Sciences
B Business
C Catering
CEA Centre for External Affairs
COM Communication Services
CS Computer Services
D Directorate
DT Design & Technology
E Enterprise
EB Estates & Buildings
EO Educational Opportunities
F Facilities
FI Finance

H Humanities
HC Health Care & Social Studies
L Library
LR Learning Resources
M Management
MAR Marketing
MS Management Services
N Nursery
P Personnel
PAY Payroll
PB Putteridge Bury
QA Quality Assurance
R Registry SC Short Courses
SS Student Services

Appendix 8 (continued)

Ms L. A. Reynolds **PB**
Mr P. T. Reynolds **PB**
Mr P. A. Rhodes **HC**
Mr B. J. Richardson **DT**
Mr I. Rivers **HC**
Ms C. Robbins **H**
Mrs C. Robinson **PB**
Mr C. J. Robinson **AS**
Mr D. Robinson **AS**
Mr D. Robinson **B**
Miss J. Robinson **E**
Ms J. Robinson **FI**
Prof K. S. M. Robinson **HC**
Mr K. W. Robinson **DT**
Mr T. Robinson **B**
Mrs B. Robson **L**
Mr D. J. Robson **DT**
Mr J. Robson **B**
Miss B. Rodgers **SS**
Mr B. Roe **B**
Mr W. Roe **AS**
Mr P. T. Rogers **DT**
Mr J. G. Rogerson **CEA**
Mr M. Rolt **DT**
Mr J. M. Rooney **B**
Mrs G. Roopra **MS**
Mr T. Ross **EB**
Mr N. H. Rowland **F**
Miss D. Ryan **P**
Miss M. Ryan **HC**
Mr G. J. Ryder **MS**

Mrs K. Sahdev **PB**
Miss K. Sahota **EO**
Mr K. G. Salmon **AS**
Mr M. Samuels **DT**
Mr C. C. A. Sanders **B**
Mrs U. Sanders-Merz **AS**
Mrs B.L. Saunders **B**
Mr M. Saunders **MAR**
Mr A. K. Sayeed **DT**
Dr K. Sayer **H**
Mr M. F. Scannell **PB**
Ms C. J. Schold-horwo **HC**
Mrs D. Schrader **EB**
Mr C. P. Scott **B**
Ms E. Scott **SS**
Mrs M. Scott **M**
Mr M. B. Scott **M**

Ms A. Scully **HC**
Mrs S. Sear **B**
Dr C. E. Seddon **AS**
Mr J. C. Sentinella **M**
Mrs J. R. Seymour **SS**
Miss A. Shah **CS**
Mr Q. C. Sharif **CS**
Mr M. Sharkey **DT**
Mrs G. Sharnock **M**
Mrs C. A. Sharp **COM**
Miss H. Sharp **P**
Mr R. A. Sharpley **B**
Dr P. A. Shaw **AS**
Mrs B. P. Shayler **C**
Mr T. W. Shenton **DT**
Mr F. Shooshtarian **AS**
Mr T. S. Short **MS**
Dr V. Shrimplin **QA**
Mr J. Shrimpton **MS**
Miss L. S. Sidey **B**
Mrs L. Simeon **C**
Mr A. D. Simmons **DT**
Mrs M. Simons **HC**
Mr D. Simpson **PB**
Mrs E. W. Singh **DT**
Mr G. Singh **HC**
Mr R. T. Skipp **AS**
Ms E. Slater **MAR**
Mr P. V. Slater **AS**
Dr R. Smalley **H**
Mrs T. E. Smart **SS**
Mr A. Smith **AS**
Mr A. J. Smith **M**
Mr B. J. Smith **C**
Miss H. D. Smith **DT**
Mr J. R. C. Smith **B**
Miss L. M. J. Smith **AS**
Mrs P.A. Smith **HC**
Mr R. A. Smith **B**
Miss S. M. Smith **D**
Mrs A. F. Smithers **HC**
Ms C. Snowden **F**
Mr C. M. Souster **B**
Miss J. Southwell **HC**
Mrs A. M. Soutter **HC**
Dr H. D. Spencer **H**
Ms S. Spindler **MAR**
Mr P. Spittles **DT**
Mr N. A. Spry **PB**

Mr A. Squire **DT**
Mrs J. Stammers **M**
Mr R. A. Stares **COM**
Miss M. D. Stearn **B**
Dr G. C. Steele **AS**
Dr J. H. Steemers **H**
Miss J. M. Stephens **F**
Mr S. Stephens **B**
Ms S. Stephens **L**
Mrs K. V. Stephenson **N**
Mrs C. Steven **AS**
Mrs C. D. Stevenson **PB**
Mrs A. E. M. Stewart **L**
Mr A. L. M. Stewart **PB**
Ms P. A. Stewart **F**
Mrs L. P. Stokes **HC**
Miss I. J. M. Stokhof **R**
Mr T. P. Stone **L**
Mr M. L. Stonnell **DT**
Mrs M. A. Storey **L**
Dr D. J. Stott **HC**
Miss K. Strachan **B**
Mr J. R. Stredwick **PB**
Miss P. C.L. Stuart **HC**
Mr G. D. Sturdy **M**
Mr G. P. Sugars **DT**
Mrs J. Summerill **F**
Mrs P. Swett **MS**
Mr A. Sword **F**
Mrs G. Sword **F**

Ms L. Tadiar **MS**
Mrs L. C. Talbot **SS**
Dr W. E. G. Taylor **AS**

Mr L. S. C. Teh **B**
Mr R. Thackwray **EO**
Dr A. M. Thody **PB**
Ms C. Thomas **H**
Mrs D. Thompson **HC**
Mr I. E. Thompson **PB**
Mr J. Thompson **EB**
Miss J. C. Thompson **PB**
Mr D. Thorne **SS**
Mrs S. Thorne **DT**
Mr D. Timms **DT**
Mrs J. Tingey **C**
Mr A. C. Tinson **AS**
Mrs E. D. Tipper **PB**
Ms B. Tirohl **H**
Mr P. L. Titterington **H**
Mr R. J. Tomlin **DT**
Mr S. W. Tomlin **DT**
Mr B. J. Tomlinson **H**
Mr M. Tomsett **EB**
Ms V. Topping **B**
Mr G. Townsend **EB**
Mr R. A. Townsend **B**
Mr M. J. Tracey **F**
Mr J. Trail **DT**
Mrs S. Tull **D**
Ms C. Turner **L**
Mrs V. F. Turner **DT**
Ms M. Turrell **EB**
Mr T. J. Twelvetree **HC**
Mr C. K. Twilley **DT**
Mrs E. Twomey **C**

Miss V. Ullah **EB**

AR Applied Research
AS Applied Sciences
B Business
C Catering
CEA Centre for External Affairs
COM Communication Services
CS Computer Services
D Directorate
DT Design & Technology
E Enterprise
EB Estates & Buildings
EO Educational Opportunities
F Facilities
FI Finance

H Humanities
HC Health Care & Social Studies
L Library
LR Learning Resources
M Management
MAR Marketing
MS Management Services
N Nursery
P Personnel
PAY Payroll
PB Putteridge Bury
QA Quality Assurance
R Registry SC Short Courses
SS Student Services

Appendix 8 (continued)

Miss P. Umradia **H**
Mrs S. Unsworth **HC**

Ms P. B. Vachon **MS**
Miss R. Vafadari **MS**
Mrs L. Vallillo **F**
Mrs D. C. Varga **MS**
Mr J. Varney **DT**
Mr C.T. Vass **EB**
Mr R. Ventham **F**
Mrs A. P. M. Verdon **FI**
Miss V. Vidal **H**
Mr S. J. Vincent **MAR**
Prof G. Vinten **B**
Miss C. T. Volpe **FI**

Mr D. D. Wade **MS**
Mrs J. Wade **MS**
Miss R. Waites **H**
Mr A. Wakeley **B**
Ms C. Walker **H**
Mrs J. A. Walker **HC**
Mr R. C. Walker **CS**
Mr S. S. Walker **F**
Mr B. R. Waller **AS**
Mrs M. E. Waller **AS**
Mr S. J. Wallman **FI**
Mrs E. Walsh **DT**
Ms H. Walsh **PB**
Mr M. L. Walters **DT**
Mrs A. Walton **PB**
Mr Y. Wang **AS**
Mr M. E. Ward **F**
Mrs M. J. Wardle **COM**
Mrs S. Warfield **B**
Mrs J. Warren **F**
Mrs L. Warren **CEA**
Mrs S. Z. Warwick **B**
Mr R. D. Washbrook **COM**
Mr A. W. Watkins **DT**
Miss E. Watkins **H**
Mrs C. A. Watson **HC**
Mrs P. A. Watson **L**
Mrs Y. M. Watson-Jones **DT**
Mr R. C. Watts **DT**
Miss E. L. Webb **P**
Mrs P. A. Webb **HC**
Mr H. F. Webber **M**
Dr A. A. Weedon **H**
Dr G. P. Weedon **AS**
Mr D. Weir **FI**
Mrs J. P. Welch **HC**
Mr G. P. S. Weller **E**
Mrs J. A. Wells **PAY**

Mrs M. Wells **B**
Mr R. Wells **EB**
Ms C. A. Wendeler **H**
Ms H. M. Wenham **HC**
Mr C. R. Westwood **DT**
Mr J. Whelan **F**
Miss P. A. White **HC**
Mr D. E. Wickens **DT**
Mr M. S. Wickens **CEA**
Mrs M. E. Wicks **C**
Mrs A. Wiggins **L**
Mr K. J. Wiggins **L**
Mrs P. R. Wilkes **B**
Miss G. Wilkinson **AS**
Mr M. D. Wilkinson **DT**
Miss N. Wilkinson **B**
Mr D. R. Williams **M**
Mrs E. Willis **E**
Mr N. R. Willmore **AS**
Mr T. Wilsher **F**
Mr A. J. J. Wilshire **B**
Mr W. R. Wilson **EB**
Mrs N. Winny **C**
Miss H. Winters **MS**
Mr R. L. Wise **H**
Mr D. J. C. Wiseman **HC**
Miss K. Wiseman **C**
Dr A. J. Wood **D**
Mr A. R. Wood **DT**
Mrs D. M. Wood **F**
Mrs S. J. Wood **QA**
Mr S. Woodhams **HC**
Mr R. P. Woods **HC**
Ms ML Worrell **HC**
Ms D. M. Worrell **PAY**
Miss S. C. Worwood **E**
Mr D. R. Wright **B**
Mrs E. Wright **C**
Dr T. V. Wright **H**
Mr K. J. Wyatt **F**
Mrs E. A. Wybrew **AS**

Mr A. Yaffe **AS**
Mr W. H. Yang **DT**
Miss K. Yeadon **B**
Miss H. A. Yon **PB**
Miss B. Young **FI**
Mr M. Young **B**
Mr M. Younis **MS**
Mr X. Yu **DT**

Dr S. M. Zakrzewski **CS**
Ms T. Zhang **CEA**
Mr D. Zjalic **AS**

Appendix 9 University of Luton Committee Structure

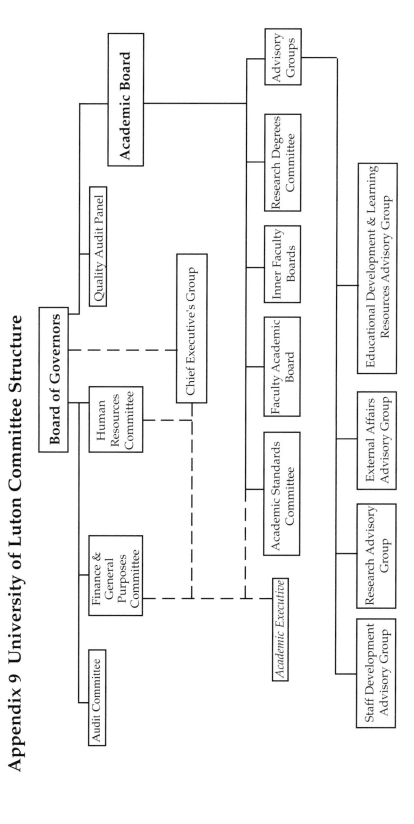

Index

A HATFUL OF TALENT